Acclaim

This book is a useful and thorough guide that is both easy to understand and easily applied.

–ROBIN LENNON, *Home Design from the Inside Out: Feng Shui, Color Therapy and Self-Awareness*

He's done it again! In direct and elegant prose, Clear Englebert has unlocked yet more secrets of feng shui.

–KIRSTEN LAGATREE, *Feng Shui: Arranging Your Home to Change Your Life* and *Feng Shui at Work*

Another easy-to-read, entertaining and inviting do-it-yourself book from Clear! Most interesting are examples from his feng shui practice that demonstrate the dos and don'ts to create love and money. Highly recommended!

–SUSAN LEVITT, *Taoist Feng Shui, Taoist Astrology* and *Teen Feng Shui*

Feng Shui expert Clear Englebert has done it again. Yet another information-packed book with easy-to-do feng shui recommendations, which will transform your life.

–ELLIOT JAY TANZER, *Feng Shui Secrets: Health, Wealth & Relationship Harmony*

An excellent primer on Western feng shui that includes effective and affordable decorative solutions to attract love and money.

–JAMI LIN, *Feng Shui Today* and Master of Feng-Shui-Interior-Design.com

This book is a direct and easy guide to maximize two central human concerns: love and money. Essential feng shui concepts are explained clearly so you know how to evaluate, fix and positively energize your home. Clear shows you exactly what you need to avoid, and what to do to improve your love life and prosperity.

–JOHNDENNIS GOVERT, *Feng Shui: Art and Harmony of Place*

I highly recommend Clear Englebert's *Feng Shui for Love and Money*! It is filled with practical teachings about the essence of feng shui cures for our relationship and money issues. These transcendental solutions are grounded in the enlightening stories from Clear's experiences throughout his many years of feng shui consultations. This book is a wonderful addition to your feng shui library.

–MASTER R.D. CHIN, feng shui architect and author, *Feng Shui Revealed*

This indispensable book is full of wonderful feng shui advice for two of the most important themes in our lives, love and money.

–SARAH BARTLETT, *The Five Keys of Feng Shui* and *Feng Shui for Lovers*

FENG SHUI
for
LOVE &
MONEY

FENG SHUI

for

LOVE &
MONEY

CLEAR ENGLEBERT

WATERMARK
PUBLISHING

ISBN 978-1-935690-71-9 (print edition)
ISBN 978-1-935690-73-3 (e-book edition)

Library of Congress Control Number: 2015945238

Book Design & Production
Dawn Sakamoto Paiva

Watermark Publishing
1000 Bishop St., Suite 806
Honolulu, HI 96813
Telephone 1-808-587-7766
Toll-free 1-866-900-BOOK
sales@bookshawaii.net
www.bookshawaii.net

Printed in the United States

Contents

Preface

About twenty years ago, I thought I was through with love. I'd had three serious relationships in my life—two that ended badly and one that ended harmoniously. I thought it was too late in my life for another relationship, and I was making plans to enter a monastery. In the meantime, I was studying feng shui and found it fascinating. (When I was in high school, I'd wanted to be an architect, until I found out that architects rarely get to design the buildings that really appeal to them.) In my little studio apartment I started working on my "Money Corner" and *wham-bam!* I quickly realized that having enough money was not going to be an issue in my life. I then started working on my "Love Corner," and it was *wham-bam!* all over again—six months later I met my soul mate. I realized I must have a knack for doing feng shui right, so I started helping my friends and it was *wham-bam!* for them, too.

My first career was as a bookseller, and through my bookstores I did some matchmaking. I'd notice when someone always came in alone and what kinds of books he or she bought. Then if another single person bought those same kinds of books, I'd introduce them. *Wham-bam!* Five marriages were made that way—three straight and two gay. Some people say they prefer to live alone, but I've found that's probably just because they haven't met the right person. Almost everyone does better in life when they've got another like-minded person to love.

Money is important, but love is much more important. May you be blessed with an abundance of both.

—Clear Englebert

Introduction

This book offers common sense feng shui advice for promoting prosperity and for attracting and enhancing relationships. Love and money are the two topics I am most frequently asked about during presentations and consultations, and they are the two components most people want to change about their lives when they turn to feng shui. Everything in life is connected to love and money—family, home, friendships, career, travel.

The far back corners in a building are the Wealth and Relationship Corners. They are of primary concern— the kinds of objects you put in those corners are of great importance for attracting or repelling energy. I will address what (and what not) to put in these areas, as well as potential problem situations (and their fixes) that commonly crop up in homes.

During a consultation, my clients often say, "That makes sense." This book will give the rationale behind every suggestion. I want you to understand the reasons for doing things. Intention is a good tool for strengthening feng shui corrections; to state your intentions you must know *why* you are implementing a fix. This book includes many real-life stories from my personal experiences and those of my clients. It's easier to see how to use feng shui in your own home when you have examples to follow, and it's the success stories that keep me practicing feng shui.

Here's one: Several years ago, I visited a dear friend in San Francisco. When she told me she was single and looking, I offered a bit of feng shui advice. We stepped into the common hall outside her apartment door, and I asked if the landlord would mind if she put something small on the dragon (right, representing masculine) side of her doorway.

"He won't even notice," she replied. I keep a few extra postage stamps with me, and one of them was a beautiful Duke Kahanamoku stamp. (He was an Olympic champion swimmer and quite handsome.) My friend stuck it on the door frame molding, and a few weeks later I got an email from her describing her new boyfriend as "hunky and sexy." I thought, *That's what I would expect using a Duke stamp.*

Apply the suggestions from this book in ways that complement your decorative style. And don't procrastinate. Changes made in a timely manner have a more profound effect than changes implemented after a delay. Procrastination dilutes the results, and feng shui is about results—go get 'em! ✍

Feng Shui Basics

Feng shui is a way of manipulating energy by the conscious placement of objects in our environment. The objects we control send out messages about how we would like our lives to work. Those messages are going out whether we intend them or not. Feng shui gives us a way to send the messages we *want* to send. The energy (chi in Chinese) that is manipulated is both the energy of our *bodies* (where we can physically move in a room or space) and the energy of our *minds* (what draws our attention).

Problems and Solutions

There are always situations in homes that are not ideal feng shui. If possible, change the situation so that the problem no longer exists—that's called a *real* fix. When you can't really get rid of a problematic object or situation, there are *symbolic* fixes, which are usually much more feasible. The appropriate fix is one that has the correct symbolism and is affordable and in keeping with your style.

Symbolic Fixes

Symbolic fixes are sometimes called cures or solutions. When it isn't possible to make an actual change, use a physical object (sometimes very small), which symbolizes your intention for change. *At the time you place the object,* say out loud what your intention is. You won't have to say that or think about it again. So whether the change you make is *real* or *symbolic,* once you've done it, just go on with your happy life.

The most common symbolic cures in feng shui are crystals, wind chimes, mirrors and the color red. It's fine to use more than one fix as long as the *rationale* for each is different, so that they are not redundant.

Crystal

A crystal represents the *dispersing of energy* because a clear, faceted crystal can indeed disperse energy—it can refract clear sunlight into rainbows. It can be a manufactured crystal (usually disco ball or octagon shaped) made of clear glass with a high lead content so that it makes rainbows in the sunlight. It can also be a natural, from-the-earth crystal but it must be quite clear or have rutilations that cause rainbows within the crystal. Keep the crystal clean so that it can sparkle. When placing a crystal, say out loud your rationale with words something like, "I am placing this crystal to disperse harsh energy from (name what the problem is) before it reaches people."

Wind Chime

A wind chime disperses the energy of the wind as sound waves and can be used instead of a crystal. (Using both a crystal and a wind chime is usually redundant and therefore only creates clutter.) But a wind chime can also *attract* energy because sound draws our attention. When we hear a sound, we look toward it. Attracting and dispersing are different ways of dealing with energy, and that's one of the reasons it's important to announce your purpose.

Mirror

A mirror can symbolize several different things, depending on its use and what you say when you install it. It is most commonly used to *reflect* harsh energy away, in which case the shiny, reflective side faces the area where the problem originates. Another use of mirrors is to expand a space, which they do by visually erasing a section of wall. We mostly use small mirrors in feng shui, but when thinking of *erasing* a wall, imagine the wall covered in one large sheet of custom-cut mirror glass. The wall would visually vanish—replaced with a view of the room. That's what symbolically happens when you use a very tiny mirror.

Any time you use a mirror that is larger than a coin there are several important considerations. Mirrors should not reflect a view of clutter, toilets or only the *bottoms* of stairs. If you can see part of yourself in a mirror, you must be able to see your head fully and completely; this is true for any adult in the household. Your image must not be distorted by such things as tinting, worn silvering or the cracks between mirror tiles. Finally, a mirror must never be positioned directly across from another mirror. If nothing else, cover one of the mirrors so they do not reflect each other.

Red

Red is the most powerful color. It's the most noticeable color to the eyes of primates, including humans. It is so noticeable that it was chosen for the color of stoplights and stop signs. Red is the color of blood, and it's used on flags more frequently than any other color. The power of red is used *to make a change* when a real change is not possible. Red is also used when there's a need to pull the eyes, and therefore *attract* energy, in a certain direction.

Yin and Yang

Yin and yang are the two divisions of the ancient Chinese system for categorizing energy and objects, with nothing being totally yin, nor totally yang. They are used to connect ideas and unify knowledge, but not to judge good and bad. The yin/yang symbolizes a very basic concept, balance—a balance that changes, yet stays even. This concept is used to create spaces that *feel* balanced, not extreme nor excessive.

Yin and yang are not fixed terms. They are relative—one thing is in *comparison* to another thing. A lake is inherently yin because it is water. Niagara Falls is water, too, but it's more yang because the water is moving quickly. An iceberg is also water, but it's more yin than the lake because the water is completely stationary. You are inherently yang because you're a living being, but you're more yin when you're sleeping and more yang when you're running.

Here is a sampling of yang and yin attributes:

Yang	**Yin**
Awake	Asleep
Active	Passive
Light	Dark
Hot	Cold
Dry	Wet
Vertical	Horizontal
Hard	Soft
Loud	Quiet
Public	Private
Fast	Slow
Simple	Complicated
New	Old
High	Low
Large	Small
Precise	Approximate

Bagua Introduction

The bagua is a nine-area grid, like a tic-tac-toe board, that lies over the floor plan of a building or a room. The areas of the bagua, each with associated elements, colors and shapes, correspond to aspects of a person's life. The most important places to apply the bagua are in the home as a whole and in rooms where you spend a lot of time, with the bedroom being the most important. It is important to apply the bagua in offices, as well as dens or living rooms if you spend time there. Don't apply the bagua to bathrooms, closets, halls, foyers and seldom-used rooms. Instead, look at where those rooms lie within the bagua of the home as a whole. It's the presence of someone *living* in a space that matters when applying the bagua.

The orientation of the bagua is based on the entrance door because that door is the most important part of any building or room. Without a door, the space is useless. For any space, the entrance door is called the mouth of energy. If the room has more than one entrance, as many living rooms do, the main entrance is whichever door is closest to the formal front door.

The bagua is oriented by the entrance wall, which has the main door somewhere along it.

FORTUNATE BLESSINGS (WEALTH)	FAME REPUTATION	RELATIONSHIP
HEALTH AND FAMILY	CENTER	CHILDREN AND CREATIVITY
KNOWLEDGE SELF-CULTIVATION	CAREER LIFE'S PATH	TRAVEL HELPFUL PEOPLE

ENTRANCE WALL

I think of the bagua as a complicated yin/yang symbol, with the most yang spaces being toward the far wall as you enter a space. The far wall has a lot of energy because it *receives* a lot of energy—it's always the first thing we see when we walk into a room. The two far corners of the back wall are the most powerful corners in a room. The two back corners of the entire home are likewise important and powerful. Even the back corners of your yard are important, as the examples will show. ✐

Love

Love comes first because it's the most important aspect of our lives.

CHAPTER ONE

Harmony

Like the still surface of a pond, harmony is considered to be the original state of things— until something disturbs the surface and makes waves. The best way to encourage harmony in relationships is to eliminate things that symbolize conflict or chaos.

Symbols of Separation and Conflict

Symbols that can represent conflict are various, but not arbitrary—there's an element of common sense in all of them. Removing (or dissipating the energy of) symbols of conflict or separation results in more harmony in your home and in your life.

Solitary Images

This is probably the most commonsense of all—avoid images of solitary people or things in your home. A solitary image says *alone*, not relating, not in harmony. This advice is vital in the Relationship Corner, which is discussed later, but it's important anywhere in the home. As consultants we are taught to be aware of "repeaters"—problems that occur more than once within a home. One single image is not a problem, but as part of a repeated theme, it'll be reflected in your life. If you collect solitary figurines, put them in groups of roughly the same height.

D-Shaped Driveway

A driveway that is shaped like the capital letter D indicates a couple who go their separate ways. It can also indicate a single person who never seems to meet the right partner. A full-circle driveway is not a problem as long as there is only one way in and out. The real solution is to reshape the driveway. If you block off one of the two entrances, do so in a way that doesn't look blocked off, but is seamless with the rest of the front yard. (For example, don't just put up a chain across the drive.) Anything that says "blocked off" represents blocked opportunities in your life.

There are three symbolic fixes. One is to place a clear, faceted crystal between the driveway and the house. Another fix is to place a small mirror at the base of the house with the shiny side facing the driveway. The crystal or mirror should be placed from knee height to ground level—low because you're reflecting back the shape of the driveway as well as the car headlights that symbolically slice into the house.

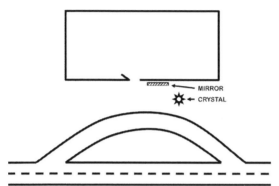

"You go your way, and I'll go mine." That's what this driveway shape suggests. A mirror and/or a crystal should be placed as indicated.

The third fix is to maintain a solid, evergreen hedge between the driveway and the house to block the harsh energy. The hedge can be a plant like boxwood or rounded-leaf holly, such as kurogane (*Ilex rotundra*) or yaupon (*Ilex vomitoria*). Leaves in the front of the home should be rounded because that shape is more welcoming than a pointy leaf shape. The hedge should be low for the same reason that the crystal and mirror are placed low. In fact, the hedge may *need* to be fairly low depending on its distance from the house. Tall hedges should be placed at least ten feet away from the front of your house. Height that close to the home has a stifling effect on the energy inside.

Stripes

Bold stripes say, "This color is my opinion, and that color is your opinion—and they stay separate." Plaids don't have that problem because there is a blending, and soft stripes where the striped colors are very similar, such as in a damask, are also not problematic. One of my clients found that when she got rid of her cabana-stripe couch pillows, not only did she and her husband argue less, but their cat stopped spraying in the house.

Clashing Knobs

If the knobs of two doors can touch each other, they represent two heads that are butting together. It's best that one of the doors be rehung so the knobs no longer touch. When that's not feasible, use the symbolic cure of red. Hang a red string, ribbon or tassel from each of the knobs that are able to touch another—this is often all four knobs. Say out loud something like, "These knobs no longer clash. This home is harmonious."

When I moved into my husband's apartment in San Francisco, the very first thing I did was to put red tassels on the knobs of the front door and the bathroom door because those knobs clashed. I asked Steve how his relationship had been with his late partner, and he admitted they had argued a lot. The apartment directly below us had exactly the same layout, and I described the occupants as "recently arrived from hell." They did not just argue, they screamed at each other at all hours—every day. Steve and I stayed harmonious, and we still are.

I once consulted for a woman in Oakland, and at the end of the consultation she wanted me to look at the part of the home that she rented out. When I saw the room, I asked, "Are there arguments here?" She looked at me as if I were psychic and said, "Arguments! How do you know that? There are always arguments here. Everybody I rent to argues in this room." I pointed out that the entrance doorknob clashed with a closet doorknob the moment the room was entered. Things that happen first are most important and set the tone for the space.

Conflicting Elements in Kitchen

Fire and water are two of the most basic elements. They are *opposite* elements, and if they are too close together or are directly opposite each other, they symbolize conflict. The sink and fridge are water, and the stove is fire. There needs to be at least a foot of counter space between fire and water appliances, and those appliances should not be directly across from each other. The location of a dishwasher is not an issue in this regard.

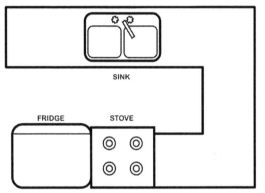

Fire and water appliances should not be too close together nor directly across from each other.

The two symbolic cures are a crystal and/or the color red. Hang a crystal between the stove and the water appliance to symbolically disperse the conflicting elements. Also, a strip of red tape can be used to symbolize a gap between the elements. The red tape can go on the bottom of a rug that's on the floor between the two appliances. Having an actual red rug there would also work. If there's no rug, there's often a small lip of countertop between where you stand and the actual sink. Put a strip of red tape under that lip extending the width of the sink. You have symbolically given the area a karate chop and created a gap between fire and water.

Microwave ovens should not be placed directly on top of, or next to, refrigerators. If there is no other option, put a board, like a wooden chopping block, directly under or beside the microwave.

Red tape is placed **under** the lip of the counter to create a separation between the water and the stove directly across from it.

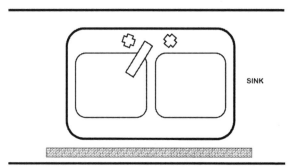

SINK

Split Views

Split views symbolize indecision or argument because one eye sees one view while the other eye sees a different view. They can occur in three problematic circumstances: near the doorway to a room, at the foot of the bed and in any room that has a freestanding column.

Through a Doorway

The doorway is the most common place for split views. When you walk into or out of a room, it's best if the wall that is directly in front of you presents one solid vertical plane, as shown in this drawing:

A solid wall should be directly across from the doorway into a room. The energy then circulates harmoniously in the room.

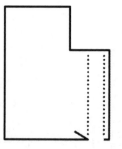

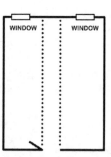

WINDOW   WINDOW

Follow the path of the door as shown in the drawing below to determine whether a wall division is directly in front of a door.

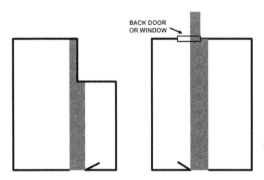

In these rooms, the energy directly from the door meets split views, which symbolize difficulty in finding agreement.

There are two solutions: a crystal or a mirror, and it's fine to employ both. Hang a clear crystal between the door and the split view. It symbolically disperses the energy that comes into or out of the room *before* it meets the split view. A small mirror placed on the wall that juts out symbolically erases that wall. The mirror must be placed on the part of the wall that is in line with the door's direct energy swath, as shown here:

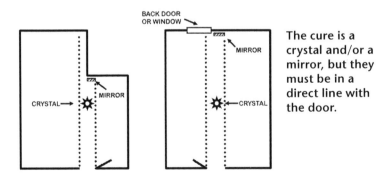

The cure is a crystal and/or a mirror, but they must be in a direct line with the door.

If you covered the entire protruding wall with a solid sheet of mirror, it would seem as if the wall were not there. That's the principle of using a mirror to erase a wall, but a very small mirror is what's usually used. The mirror can be placed on the wall behind a picture or wall ornament.

Around a Freestanding Structural Column

This kind of column is sometimes just called a pole. It's a column in a living space that you can walk all the way around, or one that rises out of an island countertop. Poles that you can walk all the way around are seen to represent *division*—we go our separate ways. You go on one side of the pole, and I'll go on the other side; we are not traveling together. Poles at the perimeter of a space, such as porch poles where the floor doesn't extend enough to invite you to walk all the way around, are not a problem.

The real cure is to put something tall next to the pole so that it's no longer a lone pole. A tall plant placed next to the pole is a common cure because it doesn't alter the traffic flow in the space. A dieffenbachia is a good choice if the pole is far from a window, because of its low light requirements. Or, you could opt for an artificial plant. Whatever you choose, make sure the leaves are round or rounded. Energy should flow smoothly around the area, and that never happens well with a spikey-leaf plant. Another real cure is to put a tall piece of furniture next to the pole. A simple room-dividing screen will work.

The symbolic cure is to put a mirror on the pole with the shiny side out and say something like, "This mirror erases this pole." If the pole has large flat sides, you can put up a full-sized mirror that's custom cut for the side. When you do that, it really does feel as if the pole has vanished, especially if all four sides are mirrored. However, most people use a very tiny mirror (smaller than a dime) tucked away discreetly under some molding.

From the Bed

The view you wake up to in the morning symbolizes your future. You need to love that view, and if there are two of you, you *both* need to love that view equally (or as close to equally as you can get). If it's a view of a dresser or chest of drawers, you both need to like what's kept on top and its arrangement. A view of a television is not ideal, and the screen should be covered when it's not on.

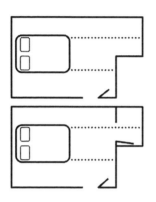

A split view from the bed can be caused by the shape of the room, or the location of a door or window.

What you *never* want is a **split view from a marriage bed**—that says, "We see different futures." The split view can be caused by a door, window or corner jutting out into the room. Use the same two cures (crystal and mirror) mentioned earlier for split views. In addition, it's a good idea to have a decorative object that extends the wall, as in the drawing below. It's ideal for the decorative object to be at least the width of the bed. Where an object on the floor would be in the way, mount something above head height, such as horizontal carved woodwork from Bali or a fabric door-top valance from India.

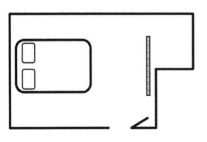

The decorative artwork can cover all or just the upper part of the split view so that you can walk under it. The couple in bed are giving themselves a unified view, which symbolizes agreement and a more long-lasting relationship.

Bed

The bed is the most important object in your home because at least a third of your life is spent there. As well as the actual bed, some of the architectural features around it can influence harmony.

Open Headboard

The best headboard is solid all the way across because that says *strength*. If it's a marriage bed, a solid headboard also says *unity*—a solid marriage. Open headboards, such as bars, slats or carved openings of any kind, indicate open relationships. The real solution for an open headboard is to replace it with a solid one, and the best symbolic solution is to make a fabric sleeve that fits over the old headboard to make it appear solid. It's also a good idea to stretch a red string from one end post of the headboard to the other and say something like, "You are now a solid headboard."

Upholstered headboards are fine because there's a solid board behind the padding. Be aware that the solid board is almost always plywood and, as with any composite wood item, *air it out well* before living with it. Composite woods are notorious for off-gassing high amounts of volatile organic compounds (VOC) that are bad for your health.

Separate Box Springs

King-size beds usually have two twin-size box springs, and the split between the box springs represents differences that are fundamental, because they have to do with our foundations. The real solution is to use a platform bed that doesn't have box springs, or switch to a queen-size bed. The symbolic solution is to put a king-size red sheet directly over the box springs while saying something like, "We are of one blood—there is no separation." Then put the top mattress over the red sheet and you'll never have to do that again because it won't get dirty.

Beam Over Bed

An exposed beam crossing lengthwise over a marriage bed represents something that divides the relationship. Hide the beam with a canopy, or hang a crystal from the bottom of the beam directly over the bed. You could also place a mirror (facing up) under the beam with the intent of reflecting the harsh energy of the beam up and away from the bed.

Cool Colors in Relationship Bedroom

A couple's bedroom should have predominately warm colors—to symbolize a warm relationship. If blue is used at all in that room, it should be only an occasional accent color. There are warm versions of most colors (even grey), but there's no such thing as a warm blue. There are no symbolic fixes for this problem—you need to shift the spectrum.

Square Windows

Square windows were not common until they began to be used in post-modern architecture. I was living in San Francisco when the new public library was built, and I noticed that *all* the windows were square. My first thought was, *Uh-oh—these folks are inviting conflict.* And sure enough, right from the get-go that library was the center of intense conflict that went on for many years. I've never heard *why* square windows symbolize conflict, but my feeling is that since all the sides are of equal length there is a lack of hierarchy, which then suggests an argumentative free-for-all.

One square window in a home is not a problem, especially if it is a picture window flanked by standard windows that are taller than they are wide. The rule is: The more square windows, the more chance of argument. To make square windows look less square, use window treatments that closely match the interior wall color. Then, when the curtains or shades are open, draw them back over the window a few inches. That will give the effect of a rectangular window.

Artwork Depicting Conflict or Chaos

Art that shows conflict or is associated with conflict is not appropriate home decor. This includes antique maps of battlefields and figurines of brawny Romans wrestling, as well as anything that feels chaotic. Chaos and harmony are quite different. One San Francisco client lived in an old building that had been converted into lofts and had at least one bare brick wall and very rough wood floors. She collected very modern art, and one of the sculptures was a single largish roll of razor wire. This was next to a chair in her living room. I made a weak attempt at asking her to get rid of it, knowing she would say no. So then I was stuck with trying to find an acceptable place for such a dangerous item. The only thing I could think of was to hang it very high at the back of the living room, so that it wouldn't be over anyone's chair and mostly out of view. She hated the idea—it had to be *in view*. We moved on to other things without resolving that because the truth is, it wasn't appropriate in a home—fine for a museum, but not a home.

If your artwork is abstract or very modern, the first question to ask yourself before displaying it is, "Does it make me feel peaceful?" If it doesn't, then don't display that piece. You can keep it as an investment, just not on display in your home.

Opposing Desks and Couches

If two desks or two couches are in the same room and directly face each other they symbolize opposing viewpoints. Chairs don't matter—they're too small. If the large, opposing furniture can be rearranged, then all is well. If that's not feasible, place a crystal on the coffee table between the couches or on one of the desks. A decorative cut-crystal object looks very natural on a coffee table. It could be a vase, candleholder, candy dish, decanter or bowl; on a desk, it could be a crystal office accessory such as a small clock, paperweight or tape dispenser. Its purpose is to disperse the opposing viewpoints, and that's what you would say out loud when placing your crystal. ✆

CHAPTER TWO

New Relationships

For a new relationship to begin or move forward, there has to be a feeling that the past has been honored and learned from, but not held onto. Then the way is open for effective symbols that you are ready and available for the right person.

Removing Old Energy

Different cultures have various ways of clearing away old vibrations that can cling to places, things or people.

Sage Smudging

To clear away old energy, some people use salt, some use citrus and some use alcohol. I use white desert sage, which is different from culinary sage. The process is called sage smudging or clearing. A great Chinese feng shui master has said that the Chinese had their techniques, but none were better than sage smudging.

Grow your own white sage if you can—it's a lovely plant. Otherwise, white sage can be bought in bundles of various sizes or as bags of individual leaves. For clearing large places such as an entire home, it's good to use a bundle. For small rooms or objects, individual leaves are usually the right size. Do the smudging in the daytime, not at night, and open all your windows, as well as your doors, if it's safe to do so. Once you've finished with the smudging, you can close them again. If you have smoke alarms, you might want to temporarily disable them. I've never made so much smoke that a smoke alarm went off—but maybe that says something about the smoke alarms. I don't travel much, but when I have to stay overnight in a hotel or condo, I always sage smudge it first thing, including under the bed. The first time I ever did that, I slept better.

Hold the stem end of the leaf or bundle, and light the tip using a candle or lighter. Since the sage has the potential to drop ash, even smoldering ash, you'll need a non-flammable bowl to hold below the sage. Blow gently on the smoldering sage to make plenty of smoke. Now take that smoke high and low. Be incredibly thorough. Let the smoke drift over and under absolutely every thing and every place. The good news is that you don't have to keep doing it over and over again. Do it once, but be thorough. If circumstances change and you feel the need, then do it again. One reason to smudge again would be after a problematic visitor has left your home.

While sage smudging, say an affirmation out loud. I like to say, "Any old vibrations have to leave now. This place (or object) is made fresh and new by the cleansing sage smoke." You can hum or sing or say prayers—it's very strengthening to use the power of your own voice at the time of a clearing. When you're done, a lot of smoldering sage may still remain, and that can be left to go out on its own in a very safe place such as a bowl in an empty sink or tub. You could also touch the sage to a bit of water, but be sure to let it dry *very* thoroughly before putting it away for future use.

Here are some examples that convinced me to believe so strongly in sage smudging:

I was asked to consult at a condo in Honolulu for a single man who had taken my classes. He'd done a good job of selecting his home, and I found very little to comment on. When we got to the Relationship Corner, he told me that the area had felt *gloomy*, and he had sage smudged it the day before. He said that within twenty-four hours he had met a woman on the Internet with whom he'd begun a promising relationship, where he previously had been unsuccessful. When referring to interest in his profile on dating sites he said, "It just exploded."

We once had a houseguest who complained of having very weird dreams while he was sleeping on our guest bed. As he described the dreams, they sounded a lot like the troubled relationship of the couple who had been our previous guests. We took his mattress into the sunlight and sage smudged it thoroughly. I was quite relieved when he reported the next morning that the dreams were gone—and they stayed gone.

I got a secondhand featherbed, and (knowing better, but being joyfully over-enthusiastic) I put it on our bed *without* sage smudging it first. I slept well, and for a light sleeper that means a lot. But after many months I woke up one morning remembering an extremely strange dream. Next night, the same thing. Over the course of a week I became very concerned about how weird my dreams were becoming. They truly felt like someone else's dreams. Then I had a dream that I was having sex with a woman. I'm a gay man, and that just doesn't happen—ever! I asked all my gay male friends, and their eyes got big like saucers and they said, "No, that just doesn't happen!"

I ripped that featherbed off our bed, and we sage smudged it like crazy and left it in the sun for the day. After that, the strange dreams vanished, and the featherbed became a neutral object. As I look back on this, I think the incident happened the way it did so that I could confidently say, "Sage works!"

The Bed

Some people think that after a relationship ends you should get a new bed and new mattress. I think that's a waste of money and resources when a little sage smoke will clear off all the old vibrations. If you really don't *like* the old bed, mattress or linens, go ahead and donate them, and get what you do like. But just because something's old doesn't necessarily mean it's bad.

Pictures

Pictures of your ex should not be on display when you are ready to invite the energy of a new person into your life. Make a respectful album or scrapbook if you want to keep the pictures—then you can visit those memories, but they won't influence your daily environment. I can't even recommend keeping pictures of your wedding to your current spouse on display—they hold you back to a moment in time and hinder your ability to move forward. Put them away in a special album. I've often seen such pictures in homes with relationship difficulties. I consulted for a family in Honolulu whose only wall decor in the master bedroom consisted of photographs from their wedding. It was obvious that those pictures weren't conducive to a good relationship atmosphere, though. He slept in that room and she slept in the room next door.

Keepsakes

Just because you own it doesn't mean you have to keep it. When a relationship is over and you feel ready to move on, revisit objects on display in your home, looking for any that are kept *only* because they remind you of that relationship. Put those objects away or let them go.

Right and Wrong Relationships

The right relationship should bring mostly joy into your life, and for it to be a long-lasting relationship, emotional maturity will be required. The other traits that I encourage are the three Cs: compassion, communication and compromise. If you are continually wondering whether you're with the right person, you're *not* with the right person. When you're with the right person, what you're thinking is, *What can I do to make their life nicer?* And usually the answer is *touch them.* My best advice on picking a partner is to get someone whose ethics are even higher than your own, and be willing to ascend.

In my twenty years as a professional feng shui consultant, I've known of a few instances where an abusive or manipulative boyfriend has left very soon after my client made changes to invite harmonious energy into the home. In every case, the woman's girlfriends came around afterwards and said things like, "How could you have *lived* with him?"

I think there are some people (usually men) who have too much anger in their life for them to feel comfortable in a home that says harmony.

The first two instances were in San Francisco, and one happened shortly after the other, so I figured I was supposed to pay attention. The first woman was into yoga and dance, and it was easy to find ways to enhance her Relationship Corner. She had some beautiful metal statues of Hindu deities, and we put a couple of the statues together in that corner. I made sure, as always, that the statues were even in height. We both agreed that it felt very natural and right. *Kapow!* The boyfriend left in the next couple of days, and then around came her girlfriends asking, "How could you…"

The second time, the result was even faster—the guy left *the next day.* The consultation for that woman will always stick in my mind. She had a huge nude portrait of herself in two parts in two different rooms. She couldn't find a way to get them both together on one wall, but that was what was necessary to create a whole image of her body on the wall. She always saw her head in one room, and in the next room she saw her naked torso. I told her that no symbolic fix would do in this instance, and we finally came to an agreement about how she could unite the paintings. I said that on the back of the paintings should be at least two red ribbons joining the two pictures, and that she should say out loud that her picture was unified and not divided in any way. Once her boyfriend left, her girlfriends came around asking, "How could you…"

The lesson in the latter instance is that you should never have images of living beings with their heads missing! Your head is what you think with, and if it's not in the picture, the symbol is that you're not thinking correctly, if at all. Beware of torso images that are missing head, arms and legs. That says, "Can't think, can't get anywhere, can't do anything." If the image is of you, the effect will be even greater.

Once, after several consultations, a client let me know that she was married but that her husband was always gone because he was in the military. She had been following my advice in the Relationship Corners of her homes, but still hadn't met Mr. Right in the bars she went to. She kept getting boyfriends she couldn't trust. Once I knew her whole story I said, "You're not going to meet Mr. Right until you have a certain physical object in your possession." She said, "I'll go right out and get it." I said, "Signed divorce papers," explaining that Mr. Right's angels were not going to let him meet her until she had those papers, because the *real* Mr. Right wouldn't mess around with a married person. In his book, *The Geography of Bliss*, Eric Weiner says, "Trust is a prerequisite for happiness... Trust—more than income or even health—is the biggest factor in determining happiness."

The reason to have a relationship is to bring more happiness into your life, not more sadness. Use feng shui to pursue not *a* relationship, but the *right* relationship.

Inviting New Energy

It's wonderful to hear back from someone that they have now met the right person, and they're so happy. Most amazing of all is seeing people, who you'd think would be next-to-impossible to match, find a mate who is just *perfect for them*. Two unique people match up successfully, and then their lives blossom. That's what I've seen repeatedly—and in my own life. I suspect it has to do with angels. You're using your home and your possessions to give out the message: "Send me the right person, please."

The right person may not be the *next* person—it took six months for it to work in my life. I arranged pink silk lotus flowers in the Relationship Corner of my studio apartment, and two seconds later my phone rang with a friend calling for a date. That quick response may have been my angel poking her elbow in my ribs saying, "This is gonna work!" Six months later I met my spouse. His ex was passing away around the time I was arranging the flowers. When I let those flowers go, I donated them to a church that used them respectfully. I don't know how else to explain it, *except* angels. I was raised believing in angels, and I've never seen a reason not to continue that belief.

The home as a whole must not be too full or cluttered if you want to send a signal to the universe that you have room in your life for a sweetheart. If you're looking for a man, don't decorate in a way that is too frilly. If you're looking for a woman, don't decorate in a way that is too minimalist. Find a happy medium between those two extremes, and you'll be more likely to find a happy spouse.

Years ago, I shocked one of my clients just south of San Francisco by asking if he was gay. He exclaimed, "No!" I said, "I didn't think so, but your home is too masculine to allow a woman to feel comfortable here." Most of the decor had to do with sports, and male sports personalities were the only people pictures he had on his walls. I explained that there wasn't a single image of a woman in his entire condo. He was hoping for a relationship, but the message of his home was that his life was filled up with sports.

Invite relationship energy with the following two specific things, in addition to enhancing the Relationship Corner as discussed in the next chapter.

Image Outside the Front Door

There are archetypal energies surrounding a home. The most basic are the tiger and the dragon. The tiger, on the left of the home as you are standing outside, facing your front door, is feminine. The dragon is masculine and to the right of the front door. If you are looking for a man, put a masculine image on the outside to the right of the door, and if you are looking for a woman, put a feminine image outside to the left of the door. You need to like the image. Avoid an image of a well-known person who everyone knows is married. It's nice if the image is visible, but in rental situations that's not always possible, so an image as small as a postage stamp or coin can be discreetly hidden. I've known this to work within twenty-four hours.

Coral or Peach Color

Yellow is the color of happiness, and pink is the color of love. Peach and coral are midway between yellow and pink. These colors say, "I'm in between, but not quite at love and happiness, and therefore *available*." Don't get out the paintbrush, because when the right person comes along you don't want to keep saying "available." Fabric is the easiest way to bring color into an area, and you can pass the fabric on to someone else once you have the relationship that's right for you. ✍

CHAPTER THREE

Relationship Corner

The Relationship Corner is to your far right when you first step into a room, apartment or house. To the far left is the Wealth Corner, discussed in Chapter Five. Those corners are located using the feng shui bagua, which is discussed on page 7.

Decorating the Relationship Corner

By decorating correctly, you are manipulating chi energy in a very powerful way. First of all, the Relationship Corner should be clean and clutter free—otherwise the energy there will be stagnant, and you won't get your best results. If clutter is a challenge in this area, be vigilant and declutter on a daily basis until the clutter is gone—*then* you can decorate!

The far right corner on the bagua map is the Relationship Corner.

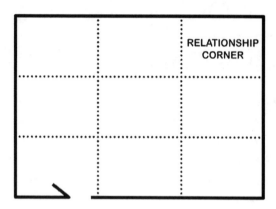

RELATIONSHIP CORNER

Colors

Pink is the color of love, and it is the most important color to have in the Relationship Corner. But large amounts of pink are not good for men. Generally, use pink only in small doses, or else use a very toned-down pink called dusty rose, which has lots of grey in it.

Other colors that are good to use in the Relationship Corner are **white**, **yellow** and **red**. Flowers come in all four of the right colors so they are one of the easiest ways to enhance this area. In the Recommended Reading section I suggest two books to help you understand the power of pink and of red.

Pairs and Groups

Don't display singular images in the Relationship Corner—have pairs or groups. As mentioned under Solitary Images, the pairs or groups should be of items that are roughly the same size. And if the decorative objects represent living things, it is very important that they not be singular. Don't hang a picture of one flower—instead display a picture of several flowers. This rule is even more important when dealing with pictures of people of your own gender. Even if it's not a photograph of you, it *still counts as a picture of you* because it's human and of your gender. One of my clients had a picture of his girlfriend in his Relationship Corner, but he said that the relationship was cooling. I said I wasn't surprised because the picture showed her alone—without him. The frame of a picture defines its world, so a grouping of separate, single images is not preferred because everyone is in their own world. An exception would be if the images were manufactured to be grouped together.

Beware of taking the above information and going on a shopping spree. You must give the symbolism of the images some thought. My preferred way of enhancing a Relationship Corner is by using objects a client already owns and likes. If someone doesn't have the right objects anywhere in their home, or if they are just itching to go shopping, I recommend silk flowers. In fact, I swear by them! Don't use flowers that have thorns, so no roses. It's not good enough to cut the thorns off the roses because roses are still famous for having thorns. There are plenty of songs associating rose thorns with love that ends up causing pain.

It's best if you buy flowers separately and arrange them yourself. Get some realistic silk flowers, and arrange them in a nice vase or basket that you also like. Take your time doing it, and do a great job. The height of the vase should be approximately one-third of the height of the highest foliage or flower. However, there are exceptional vases in which that rule doesn't apply. Don't use ikebana arrangements in the Relationship Corner if they employ a metal pincushion holder. That kind of flower holder is fine in other areas of the bagua, but not in the Relationship Corner because of the sharp points.

I have a client in northern California who consults with me every so often, long-distance. She emailed me:

> Walked the property to ascertain relationship area. Within an hour my husband asked me out on a romantic dinner date and made me breakfast the next morning—something he only does once a year or so (breakfast, that is). His crabbies are gone! Oh, why? Found a single cement goose who used to be a pair. The other one broke so I made sure to pitch it. It was somewhere else, and it got moved at some point into relationship area. Oops. Also, two people who are normally huffy at me (and the world) at work have been much nicer.

Another success story: I have a surfer friend who was great with waves, but horrible with relationships. His small home was totally undecorated, and I suggested he take smooth stones from the beach and put pairs of them in the Relationship Corners of each of his rooms. He did so and soon surprised me by bringing his new girlfriend by to meet me. He met her at the beach, and they're quite happy together after several years. Since he's determined to make this last, he's finally learning some relationship skills.

Romantic Decor

Decorate any Relationship Corner with at least a few objects that are *your version* of romantic. Your version of what feels romantic doesn't have to look anything like Martha Stewart's interpretation. You're the one who lives there; make it your style. It's been my repeated experience that when the enhancements are very personally meaningful, the result is more profound.

Hearts

Hearts are the most common symbol of love, but beware of having only one heart all by itself—it's a lonely heart. Just as bad is two hearts of very different sizes—that says one heart contains more love than the other heart—quite sad. Also, beware the material they are made of. Wood is good because it's not as hard as stone, but more durable than fabric. Avoid plastic hearts because of the material's connotation as fake or imitation. Nobody wants fake love.

I consulted twice for a woman who did some shopping between my visits. On my first visit, I suggested that she make her Relationship Corner more romantic. When I came back she showed me the small glass hearts she had bought and put in glass dishes on the coffee table in the Relationship Corner. One container had clear hearts, and another had red hearts. The hearts had rounded edges. She said she loved to dig her hand down into them and proceeded to demonstrate. It looked as if she was dipping her hand into small heart-shaped ice cubes. I told her that it was fine to keep the red ones since ice cubes aren't red, but that the clear hearts seemed cold and icy. Glass can suggest brittleness and something easily broken, but that wasn't the case in this instance.

The Word "Love"

I don't recommend using the word "love" in its written form in the language you usually speak in the Relationship Corner. If you have the word written only once, it's a lonely love, but if it's written twice it can make an area look too busy. An exception would be a pair of smooth small stones with the word "love" carved into each one, positioned snuggled up, touching each other.

Plants

A houseplant can be romantic—*or not*. Plants with stiff pokey leaves are definitely not romantic, nor are plants with thorns, barbs or irritating bristles. Plants with fuzzy, rounded leaves are ideal, such as the velvet leaf, also known as the purple passion plant (*Kalanchoe tomentosa*) or even velvet plant (*Gynura aurantiaca*) with leaves that aren't as rounded, but still so approachable that you want to stroke them with your finger. Artificial plants are fine here as long as they aren't known for thorns, like roses.

Plants with pink flowers are perfect, so if you have a sunny window here, begonias or geraniums would be appropriate. Sweetly fragrant plants are also wonderful in this area. There are suggestions for fragrant-plant books at the end of Recommended Reading. Climbing plants can be problematic because they cling and need support, and those characteristics aren't healthy in relationships. The right philodendron could be just fine here if there are also several other *upright* plants nearby. Two good philodendrons are velvet-leaf vine (*Philodendron micans*) and heart-leaf philodendron (*Philodendron scandens*). If you have a yard, it would be best to have the appropriate kinds of plants (especially thorn-free) in the far right corner of your back yard.

Collections

Collections are usually very appropriate in Relationship Corners, but even collectibles have to be scrutinized carefully for their symbolism. One woman collected Snow White and the Seven Dwarves figurines and pictures, but not one scene had the Prince in evidence. She was single, and I suggested she start collecting pictures showing the Prince, especially if they were to be placed in a Relationship Corner. Weapon collections should never be in a Relationship Corner, and that includes kitchen knives, which can be in a Relationship Corner if absolutely necessary, but *not* on display. (The topic of feng shui and collecting is vast and a particular interest of mine since I'm an avid collector—and I certainly don't view a well-maintained collection as clutter.)

Objects with Relationship Energy

Ordinary household objects have *relationship energy* when it's obvious that several things are put together to create the object—woven baskets, for example. A pedestal table doesn't have as much relationship energy as a table with four legs. A pole lamp that is one metal pole doesn't have any relationship energy. It clearly says, "One—I'm all alone." Some pole lamps have four legs that join together, then twist and make interesting patterns as they rise to the lightbulb. And any lamp with more than one bulb has more relationship energy than a lamp with a single bulb.

Earth Element

Since earth is the element in the Relationship Corner, it's very appropriate to have objects made of earth placed here. For example, a glass jar with layers of multicolor sand, stone sculptures or pottery. Vintage pottery is my favorite choice because it's romantic and varied enough to accommodate anyone's taste. I visited an old friend in my Alabama hometown who collects vintage mid-century items. He used to have two kiosks in antiques malls, but no longer retails. However, he has not stopped buying, and his house was crammed with what used to be for sale, as well as what he continued to amass. I like mid-century items, and as I looked around his house I noticed a pink pottery television lamp (popular in the 1950s) depicting two doves, with gold highlights. I suggested that it be placed in the Relationship Corner of the house, which was the laundry room. He said, "Go ahead, if you can find room." I *made* room because I knew how perfect that lamp was for enhancing relationship energy. A few days later he said, "That feng shui sure does work fast! A guy just gave me his phone number, and I've been trying to get his number for *ten years!*"

Earth is represented by yellow, or any earth tone, and the shape for earth is square or horizontal rectangular.

Broken or Stuck Objects

Don't keep broken objects in a Relationship Corner, and don't put anything there that is made up of broken pieces, such as mosaic art. Years ago, one of my dear friends was showing me around her yard. I discovered the Relationship Corner was where she kept broken pottery for mosaic making. I was aghast and said she really needed to find a different place to store the broken pieces. I reinforced my point by singing the refrain from "Breaking Up is Hard To Do." Well, I guess she thought the pottery too much trouble to move, and she didn't follow my advice. Shortly thereafter, her husband left her for another woman, and she has never gotten over it. Be conscious of what you are asking for—that's one of the basic premises of feng shui.

Here's another story: I consulted for a couple in a very expensive, modern home, and I was shocked to see that the dining table and bar top were made of glass that looked as if it were shattered. I told them that the symbolism of its looking broken did not bode well, but the wife insisted it was the latest thing; they were going to keep it and wouldn't consider covering it. That marriage didn't last one more year.

Blocked doors represent blocked opportunities, as do windows that are stuck and won't open. Squeaky hinges and dripping faucets are fairly easy to deal with and should be repaired. If a broken or stuck object is in your Relationship Corner (or anywhere in the home) and there's absolutely nothing you can do about it, put a tiny red dot on the problem, and say out loud, "You're not broken (or stuck). You're fixed."

Bare Glass Edges

Another rule that holds true for *every* bagua area: No tables or shelves with **bare glass edges**. They have a severe cutting energy that cuts you off from achieving your goals related to whatever area they are in. So if a table with a bare glass edge is in your Relationship Corner, it's hampering your relationship energy. If it's in the Wealth Corner, it's your prosperity that's being damaged. Imagine a razor-sharp glass Frisbee moving around in your home—that's how serious the problem is. I did not want to believe that when I first studied feng shui. I had two glass shelves in my Fame Area, and I really liked them there. As I kept studying, the same thing was repeated—watch out for bare glass edges. I finally wrapped them in paper and put them in a closet, thinking I could put them back if I didn't like the results. The results were incredible—I was *asked* by a publisher to write my first book. My website was given to me for free. I got rid of those shelves and have never looked back.

If the glass has a rim around it, there is no problem, and if the glass doesn't extend beyond the tabletop that it's sitting on, there is no problem. It's only a problem when the bare edge extends into the room. You can cover the table or shelf with a cloth and the problem is solved. Even a lace tablecloth is fine. There is a product made for car doors, which works well for rimming bare glass edges if the glass is fairly thin. (See Sources.)

Televisions

Televisions are inappropriate in the Relationship Corner because we don't use them to relate; in fact, the opposite happens—when the TV goes on, relating stops. If a TV must be in a Relationship Corner, it should be covered or out of view when it is not turned on. Put it behind doors or drape fabric over it. Any fabric used should be the correct colors for this area. Computers and telephones are fine because we use those devices to connect to others.

Missing Relationship Corner

An area of the bagua can be missing if the house is not a perfect square or rectangle. If some or all of the far right corner of the home is missing, it's going to be a lot harder for the residents to find or maintain relationships. A missing corner occurs where the missing area is half (or less) of the entire outside length of the back of the house. There can also be a missing area in a room, such as when a small closet juts into a room. When an area is missing in the house as a whole, it's especially important to enhance that area within individual rooms.

The Relationship Corner is mostly missing because the far right corner is not included in the floor plan.

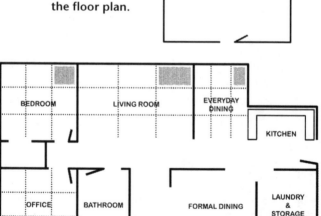

The Relationship Corner is partially missing in this home. But there are four rooms in which to emphasize the Relationship Corner within those rooms.

There are two ways to bring back a missing corner—do both if possible. Place one or more mirrors on the inside wall or walls that are tangent to the missing area. The reflective part of the mirror shines into the room. The mirrors symbolically enlarge the home. The other solution is to mark the apex of the missing area with something significant. The apex is the point outside where the walls on the two sides of the house would meet if the house were fully rectangular. Since we're talking about the Relationship Corner, what is used to mark the apex of the corner should be something that shows relating, such as two rabbit figurines placed together. It would be best to use objects made of natural materials (including cement) rather than plastic, because plastic can say artificial.

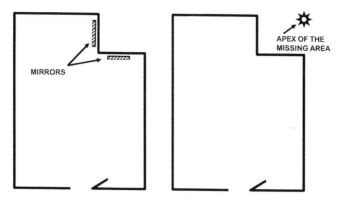

Put mirrors on the inside walls that are tangent to the missing area, and mark the apex of the missing area with a significant object.

Years ago, I consulted for a woman in Palo Alto who had said over the phone when she was arranging the consultation, "I want a man!" I asked a bit about the shape of her house and then told her that I thought she had a missing Relationship Corner. She quickly responded, "I know my feng shui. I don't have any missing corners—I have an *extension* in my Fame Area." I bring a measuring tape to all my consultations, and sure enough, when the walls were measured she had missing Wealth and Relationship Corners. To make matters worse, the apex of the missing Relationship Corner was in the middle of the driveway which curved back behind the house to a detached garage.

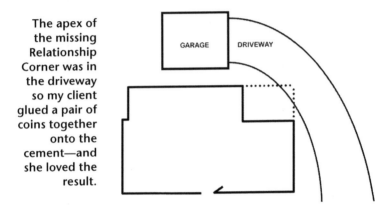

The apex of the missing Relationship Corner was in the driveway so my client glued a pair of coins together onto the cement—and she loved the result.

GARAGE   DRIVEWAY

I'd never encountered this situation before, and hadn't heard it referred to in any books I'd read, so I stood there scratching my head trying to think what to suggest. Finally it came to me, "Get two coins of the same size, one with a man's image on it and one with a woman's image on it. Glue them face-to-face as if they're talking to each other, then glue them down on the driveway. They won't hurt your tires."

Her face lit up and she exclaimed, "I love that! I've got a foreign coin collection, and it'll be so much fun to go through them to pick ones that are meaningful to me." I saw her again at a book signing several months later, and she was eager to share her story: "I've been meeting the highest quality men I've ever met in my life—and get this, buddy, they're all foreign!" We both laughed. It proved once again that you get what you ask for.

If the room that is in the Relationship Corner of the house is a room that you rent out to people, then it should be considered a missing area, and you'll only be able to do one of the cures—the mirrors inside the home.

Extension

An extension is the exact opposite of a missing area. An extension is a small part of the house (or room) that bulges out; and that bulge gives extra oomph to the area of the bagua in which it occurs. An extension is less than half the full length of the side of the house. If you wonder whether your place has an extension or a missing area, err on the side of assuming it's missing. At least use mirrors to symbolically enlarge and even out the shape of the floor plan.

This house has an extension in the Relationship Corner, which is excellent for relationship energy.

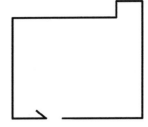

Missing Masculine Corner

The Relationship Corner is the *feminine* corner of the bagua, and the *masculine* area (commonly known as the Helpful People/Travel Area) is the close right corner in a home. Bringing back a missing Relationship Corner not only makes a home more receptive to relationship energy, but it makes the home easier to live in for a woman. If the home has a missing masculine area, the male energy is symbolically gone. This can happen where a carport or garage juts into the floor plan of the house. I've often seen this type of home where a widow is living—the masculine corner is gone, and so is the man.

To bring back a missing masculine area, use one or more mirrors as directed in the previous section. The object that is placed at the apex of the missing area should be masculine in some sense, such as a coin with a man's image on it. Coins are especially appropriate in this area because metal is the element here, and round is the shape that represents metal.

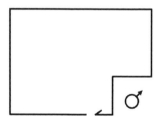

The close right corner of this home (or room) is missing. Since that's the masculine corner, the home does not invite or support male energy.

Very Irregular Floor Plans

Some homes and many apartments have very irregular floor plans, and your job is to make them symbolically square or rectangular. I err on the side of assuming an area is missing if it feels like it *might* be missing. The following drawings are of actual apartments and they show where I would put mirrors, just to be on the safe side. ✎

The dotted lines show where the corners would extend to, if these apartments were complete rectangles.

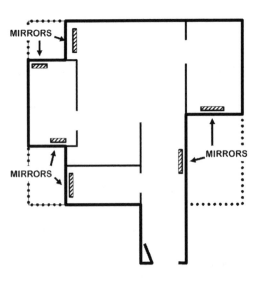

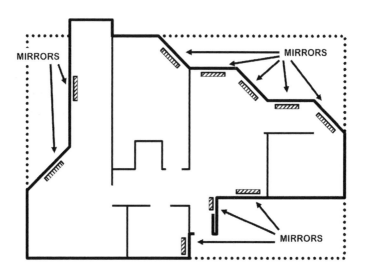

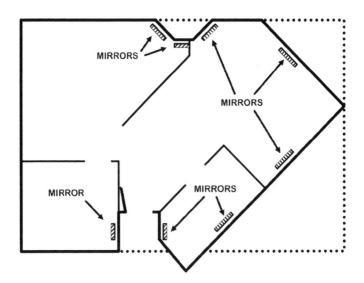

Money

It can't buy love or happiness, but it sure pays the bills.

Chapter Four

How Prosperity Finds You

Prosperity begins at your driveway and ends at your toilet—and much can happen in between.

The Site and Its Approach

How energy *finds* you is a primary concern in feng shui. It's the first thing that happens, and first things are most important. The best approach feels easy and logical, and the ideal home site feels protected and retains energy.

Road and Driveway

The road leading to your property and your driveway should be as smooth as is feasible—definitely no potholes or big rough bumps. A rough road leading to your door symbolizes good fortune bouncing off before it reaches you. If smoothing out the road or driveway isn't possible, use the symbolic cure of the color red. Put a tiny drop of red paint or nail polish in every pothole or bump, and say out loud, "You're smooth and flat now."

I consulted for one of the wealthiest families on Hawai'i Island. The thing I first noticed when I turned off the road was the incredible driveway. It was totally smooth cement and went on curving around for miles. I kept thinking, *No wonder they're wealthy, with a gracious driveway like this!* It definitely invited prosperity.

Stairs to Door

If there are stairs going up to your front door, they must be closed-riser stairs. Open-riser stairs allow energy to pass between the treads; therefore, less energy reaches your front door. The real solution is to install something connecting the treads. Boards are best, but it's fine to use whatever is safe and works. An artist client used oilcloth, usually sold as a cover for outdoor tables. She chose a Mexican floral with lots of red in it—she stapled it up herself, and her career shot up within a week.

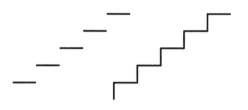

Open-riser stairs do not allow energy to fully reach your door. Closed-riser stairs are ideal because they allow energy to ascend to your front door.

Some stairs (usually cement and metal) have no risers, and it's not feasible to add them. The very best symbolic fix is to *safely* add red to connect the bottom floor to the upper floor level. Apply a thin line of red paint, and take care to make the red line continuous. There's also a way to do this with red cotton thread, but be sure to do it safely. The thread goes along the bottom of the stair support beam, because you never want to run the risk of the thread coming loose and tripping someone at night. This fix is not feasible when the stairs are common property leading to apartments. In that case, your very best option is to make the outside of your front door area look as noticeable as is allowed. Wind chimes and the color red are ideal. A red doormat or a red tassel hanging from your doorknob are often allowed by apartment managers.

Front Door Area

Painting the outside of the front door red is standard feng shui advice, but if your front door stays open a lot for air circulation, the outside of the screen door should be what's painted red. Red is not an appropriate color on the entrance wall *inside* the home. (Dark colors, even black, are preferred along the inside of the entrance wall.) The front door and area around it need to jump into view as soon as someone has arrived at your home. There must be no mistaking where the front door is—it should be both **visible** and **unmistakable**.

If your front door doesn't have *both* of those characteristics, you do need some **red** on it or around it. A rich bright **yellow**, such as is used in the center of roads, is also perfect if red will not harmonize with the colors that are already in place outside your front door. If you have a nicely stained wood door, I don't recommend painting it, but find a way to incorporate red (or yellow) very close to the door—a brightly colored doormat is a nice choice.

A front door that is not immediately apparent to a first-time visitor symbolizes energy missing you, and some of that energy is money. Take this situation seriously and use signage and/or a very obvious smooth sidewalk leading to the front door. Near the door, hang a wind chime, announcing that entrance to the world. If your style is exuberant, this is your opportunity to let loose. It would be hard to overdo it. For people who would rather avoid gaudiness, consider consulting with a design professional, and keep repeating to them, "Noticeable, noticeable, noticeable."

I consulted for a client who had a yellow front door, and at the end of the consultation I complimented him on the door because yellow is my favorite color. "However," I said, "I would be failing in my duty if I didn't mention that red is the *preferred* color for the outside of the front door." He quickly followed that advice and reported back that within hours thousands of dollars started pouring his way via the Internet, where he made his living.

Adequate Back Yard

Prosperity is considered to accumulate in the back yard. Think of a drawstring purse with coins coming in through the opening (on your property that's where the driveway meets the road) and building up at the bottom of the purse. Your back yard symbolizes the bottom of the purse, and if it's not at least as large as the front yard, there's not an adequate area for prosperity to build up. If your back yard is quite small compared to your front yard, symbolically enlarge it with mirrors. Put one or more mirrors (any size) at the very back of your yard, facing toward your property. Say out loud something like, "This mirror is symbolically enlarging the back yard so there's more room for prosperity to accumulate."

Apartment dwellers don't have yards, and that's neither a pro nor a con. They simply don't have the issues that come with maintaining a yard. Yards themselves can be advantageous or disadvantageous, depending on how they are maintained. The issue of "accumulating wealth" concerns the back part of what you own. If you don't have a back yard, it's the back part of your unit. In an apartment, where the back wall might be made up entirely of windows, put something very heavy—like a stone table, which represents *grounding*—in this area.

Moneybag Lot

If the sides of your property splay out toward the back, there's even more room for prosperity to accumulate. That's called a *moneybag lot*—very auspicious.

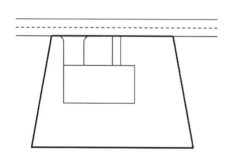

Your driveway and sidewalk are the mouth of your property; they are where prosperity enters. They correspond to the opening in a drawstring purse, and this lot shape is called moneybag because there's plenty of room for money to build up in the back.

Wind

Too much wind around your home chips away at your prosperity. The best choice is to move to a more sheltered location. *Move* is one of the four-letter words that I try never to say, but in this circumstance it is truly the best option. Especially if you are a skinny person, constant forceful wind is not good for you. (For more information on the effect of wind on slender people, see *Perfect Health* in Recommended Reading.) Breezy times are good for the energy of a home—they keep it from being stagnant. But in places where high winds are more than occasional, long-lasting prosperity is elusive.

If moving is truly not an option, plant an evergreen windbreak. There can also be a fence, but the growing plants are *essential*. They defy the wind with the upward growing force of their life. Needless to say, the plants should be as erect as possible.

Water and its Symbolism

Water symbolizes prosperity. Colors and shapes that symbolize water or flowing energy also symbolize wealth. The colors for water are blue (the blue ocean) or black (a dark well). The shape for water is wavy or freeform.

Real Water

The position of real water near your home is important to your finances, and if the water moves, the direction of the flow is important. The flow can be in all directions, like an umbrella, but if the water flows in only one direction, like a waterfall, the flow should be toward the front door or the heart of the home. The best place for any water feature, natural or human-made, is the front yard, not the back yard. In the front, it represents bounty ready to flow in your front door. In the back, it represents an abyss that your home is sliding into—lack of support, including monetary support. If there's a water feature in the back, put a mirror and/or a crystal between the home and the water. The mirror reflects *at* the water and symbolically moves its influence away from the home. The crystal symbolically disperses the influence of the water before it reaches the home.

Blue Roof

Your roof can be any color *except blue.* The purpose of the roof is to shed water away from the home, so when the roof is blue—the color of water and prosperity—that's wealth flowing *away* from the home, not into it. Repaint the roof a different color if you can, but since that's not usually possible, there are two symbolic cures—use one or both.

A clear, faceted crystal can be placed on a ledge or shelf above head height inside the home. Say out loud words to this effect: "This crystal disperses the effect of the blue roof before it affects the people in the home." The other cure is a mirror (any size) placed above head height with the shiny side facing up. It can even be glued to the ceiling with the back painted to match the ceiling color so it isn't noticeable. Say something like this: "The purpose of this mirror is to reflect away the influence of the blue roof. Money does not flow away."

Black can also represent water, but not in roof color. Black just doesn't stand out color-wise as blue does on a roof. A blue roof is always very noticeable.

Wavy Lines on Front Gate

Not all properties have or need gates, but if you do have a driveway or walkway gate, there are three designs to be cautious of. *Wavy lines* represent ripples or waves on water. When that kind of design is on your front gate it symbolizes money flowing out your driveway. This is especially serious when the gate is at a lower elevation than the house. You can put a discreet dot of red paint on each wavy bar and say, "You are flat; you are not wavy." However, it's best to change the design of the gate. Don't use a *zigzag* (herringbone) pattern, which symbolizes things going up and down, not remaining steady. The design should be inviting, even though the purpose of the gate is to keep people out, so avoid bars that look like upright spears with *spear points* on each pole. If nothing else, put a ball on each point. Other than those three cautions, feel free to make your gate or gates very charming and beautiful. Incorporating red into the design makes it even better.

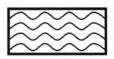 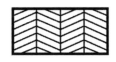 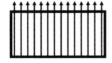

Don't use these designs on your front gate.

I met a gentleman from India in the lobby of his hotel in San Francisco, and as he showed me the layout of his home compound, I asked about his gate color. He said, "Black," and I got the impression that everybody's gate was black. I suggested that he paint it red. His eyes got big and he said, "*No*body in India has a red gate!" I said, "Good, it'll be noticed."

Half-Circle Doormat

Outside doormats should be rectangular. The half-circle shape is fine for use indoors only, never outside. The reason is that the half-circle shape is like the spout of a measuring cup where water could be poured out. The symbolism of water pouring into your home is fine, but if the spout shape of the half circle is *outside* any door of your home (not just the main front door), the symbolism is that money is being poured out of the home.

Within the Home

If you live in an apartment or condo, you probably don't have control over the outside, but once you're inside your home, it's your territory—and your responsibility. You get what you ask for, so be aware of the message that your possessions are sending out.

Drains

Since water represents money, a drain represents money *leaving* your home. All drains are problematic, and the toilet is the most problematic since the drain hole is the largest in the home. Keeping bathroom doors closed is the *first step* toward fixing this problem. Then your subconscious is not influenced by seeing the fixtures, which have drains. You just see a door and that's all—it looks the same as a closet door or a bedroom door. If the bathroom has no door, either install one or put up floor-length curtains.

Lid Down

When you're not using the toilet, keep the lid down. That's a simple way to solve a very big problem. However, don't put a sign on your toilet asking guests to close the lid. It's enough that you do so, and ask other household members to. I highly recommend the toilet lids that slowly close themselves when the open lid is gently nudged downward.

Circle of Red

One remedy for the symbolism of money draining away is to put a circle of red around the drain under a sink. Red paint, tape or string represents a karate chop—the drain is cut away. Say out loud something like, "This drain is cut off—no financial drain."

Mirrors

Small mirrors are also a good way to keep the influence of a drain confined so that it doesn't influence the rest of the home. The shiny side of the mirror faces toward the drain. This is especially important if a stove, desk or bed is directly on the other side of the wall or floor from a drain.

In the illustrations below, the left side drawings show examples of mirror placement within the bathroom, and the right side drawings show the locations for mirrors in the adjacent room. I recommend putting mirrors in both rooms. The mirrors in the bathroom keep a large amount of the drain energy confined in that room. The mirrors in the adjacent room prevent the energy of *the drainpipes in the wall* from coming into a room that has a bed, desk or stove. The shiny side of the mirrors in the adjacent room face the wall. It's fine to use a small mirror, or you can use several squares of mirror tiles to do a more complete job of covering the area of the drain pipes. You can paint over the back side of the mirror that shows in the room.

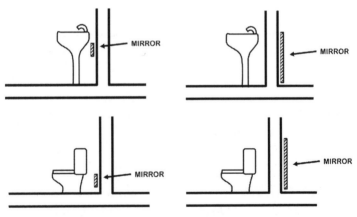

The reflective side of the mirror faces toward the drain, reflecting the drain away from the adjacent room.

The reflective side of the mirrors faces the wall, keeping the drain energy confined to the bathroom.

For shower and tub drains, put mirrors on the wall of the next room that is adjacent to the drain. Measure, if necessary, to locate the mirrors correctly. The reflective side should face the wall. While affixing it, say something like, "This mirror reflects away the drain energy so it does not affect my finances."

A mirror is used when a drain is directly above or below the **entrance door**, or the three other important places—around the **bed**, **desk** or **stove**. Put a small mirror on the ceiling of the lower room. The reflective side faces up if the drain is above, and down if the drain is below. When the drain is below, you can put the mirror on the floor of the room above if you're sure it won't get broken. An example: When a toilet is below the bed, a mirror can be placed under the bed with the reflective side down. The mirror can be any size, even full length. Drains above or below the four important places are thankfully not common because efficient architects try to put drains above or below other drains, so bathrooms are often above other bathrooms.

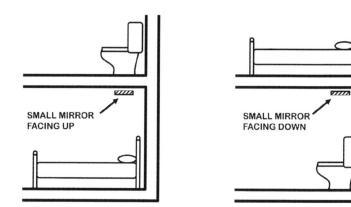

SMALL MIRROR FACING UP

SMALL MIRROR FACING DOWN

The reflective side of the mirror faces up at the ceiling when the drain is above, and the reflective side faces down when the drain is below you.

Heavy Object

A third way to counteract the influence of a drain is to put a very heavy object directly under or beside the drain. A twenty-pound barbell weight is good for putting in the cabinet under a sink because it's flat and you can still store items on top of it. Say out loud that you are grounding your good fortune so that it doesn't slip away.

Clutter

An over-crowded home sends out a very clear message—"Don't bring me more bounty, I wouldn't know what to do with it. I can't handle what I've got now!" With that in mind, *make time* to deal with cluttered spaces. Turn the television off and don't turn it back on until your home is clutter-free. You also need to change habits of acquisition. One gentleman was going to drive me home after the consultation at his house. When we got into the garage, he slapped his forehead and pointed to a pile of objects. "We completely forgot to ask you where to put these things. We just bought them yesterday." "Well, where did you intend to put them when you bought them?" I asked. He replied, "We didn't have any idea—we just liked them and bought them." I said, "That's called *indiscriminate consumption,* and you shouldn't do that." He looked ashen and said, "We've got two houses filled like that."

Clutter is a problem anywhere in a home or business, but when it's in a Wealth Corner, it's deadly for finances. ☙

CHAPTER FIVE

Wealth Corner

The common name for this area is the Money Corner or Wealth Corner, and that's how I usually refer to it, rather than saying the longer and more correct name— Fortunate Blessings Area. However, it's important to remember that fortunate blessings can take many forms that don't directly involve money. The location of this corner is derived from the feng shui bagua, which is discussed on page 7.

Decorating the Wealth Corner

The Wealth Corner is in the far left corner as you enter the home or into any room where you spend a lot of time, such as your bedroom. A studio apartment has only one Wealth Corner, and it's very powerful since all the living is done in that room. Do the right feng shui in a small place like that, and you'll probably find yourself in a larger home before too long.

The far left corner is the Wealth Corner.

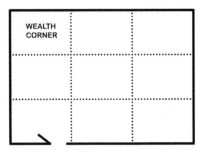

The Wealth Corner should be clutter-free and tidy, with clean windows. This is the wrong place for an open trashcan—if the can must be there, it should have a lid. Avoid bare glass edges in your Wealth Corner, and don't keep broken or malfunctioning objects in this area. If the Wealth Corner of the home is a child's bedroom, it's important to have a picture of the parents or head(s) of the household on the wall in that room. Otherwise, the child can become too powerful in the home.

Colors

Purple is the color of wealth. **Green**'s good too—think of the greenback dollar. **Red** and **blue** are also good colors for the Wealth Corner. You certainly don't have to use them all; I hope that you don't—the result could be an eyesore. Pick one or possibly two of the colors that you think would look good together in the far left corner of your space and use *rich* tones of that color. If you're planning to paint a wall or two anyway, the glory of paint is that it costs no more to add some pigment. Then you've got a nice big dose of the right color in your Money Corner. Consider giving it a try. Live with the right color in the right area for six months, and you'll probably love the *result* so much that you wouldn't consider painting over it.

Purple

Purple's not for everyone, and if it's not for you, please skip on down to the next color. If you already like purple, or think you could be talked into it, read on. Purple is the color of royalty. That was the case in ancient China and in ancient Rome; in both cultures *only royalty* were allowed to wear purple. The island that produced purple dye (from seashells) was left off of the ancient Roman maps of the Mediterranean so that emperors could maintain their monopoly of the color.

Purple doesn't go well with many other colors, but it looks great with yellow, green, beige, pink or white. Blue and purple are not a good combination, and black with purple is too somber. Violet is a fiery purple, with more red and less blue, and is quite an appropriate option.

If it's in keeping with your style, I highly recommend painting an accent wall purple in the Wealth Corner of your bedroom and/or the Wealth corner of the whole home. I got this email from a client several years ago:

> You came to our house to do a consult right after we moved in and suggested that I paint a wall in my bedroom red or purple—it was the wealth corner of the house and also the wall that connected the wealth and relationship corners in my room.
>
> Well, I painted the wall a deep, vibrant purple and a number of things happened:

- We sold the house for almost three times what we paid for it

- I became romantically involved with a friend

- My son-in-law got an offer to work

Green

Green is one of the colors I recommend most frequently for interiors. While a light sage green is restful to live with, the purpose of green in the Wealth Corner is to look *rich*, so use a vivid hue such as forest green, Kelly green, or emerald green. One of the nicest things about green is that various shades of it rarely clash with each other—so mixing and matching greens can look as natural as different leaves in the forest.

Red

The most important thing to remember about red tones used in the Wealth Corner is that they should be *fiery*, not earthy. Use bold reds such as crimson or scarlet. Bold does not have to be brash—there are also rich, sophisticated reds like oxblood red and Chinese red.

A mortgage broker called me to consult for her firm. I had consulted for them when they first opened ten years before, and I was pleased to hear she wanted some different colors. Previously, we had put a rich green on the back wall, and this time I was hoping I could talk her into red. It's often difficult to talk someone into a rich red wall. That wouldn't be my recommendation in most homes—but in an office situation, red on a distant back wall looks energizing without being overpowering. The large painting that was to stay in the center of the wall had a good bit of earthy red, but there was a very rich true red in a few small places, and that's what we tried to match. It worked like a charm. Even before she reopened, people were looking in the window, then coming in to say how beautiful the colors were. We had picked a light, greyish almond color for the other walls in that room, and the result was magnificent. The trim was pure white, which looked clean and crisp and didn't interfere with the other colors.

A most amazing use of red inside a home was in an old San Francisco Victorian building. The couple had painted the back wall of the bedroom a very sophisticated red, a very deep red. My first words were, "How many coats?" They said, "Five, and in some places six." It does take more than one coat to get saturation with the color red. This was ultra-saturation, and there was a frieze along the top foot of the high wall. They had taken lines from an Antonio Machado poem and stenciled them in large letters so that you read it by turning fully around in the room. The words were something like, "I dreamed there were bees, and they were taking all the foibles and troubles of my life and making honey and honeycomb." It was one of the most wonderful rooms I've ever been in.

Blue

Blue does not usually go well with green, so it's safest to pick one or the other. Cobalt blue and royal blue are some of the best blues for this area because they're the *richest*. Blue glass is appropriate here, as is ruby glass. Don't paint a bedroom blue if a couple sleeps there because it's a cool color symbolizing a cool relationship.

What if your refrigerator is in your Wealth Corner? Having that very boring, functional appliance in that particular area was the predicament of one of my San Francisco clients. To enhance the area, I recommended she replace the refrigerator with one that was cobalt blue. She jumped at the opportunity because she was planning to replace the fridge eventually. The next time I consulted for her, it was at her new chiropractic office, which was several times larger than her previous one. She doesn't regret the pretty penny she paid for the blue fridge—her practice has continued to prosper. Any fridge in a Wealth Corner should be kept shiny and free of magnets and notes.

Another room that may be a challenge to "dress up" when it's located in the Wealth Corner is a laundry room. I told one client to make hers look royal, and she quickly went to work using purple carpet tiles and extravagantly beautiful pictures. She said that within a few hours she got a call from someone asking her to manage a vacation rental, which she described as the most lucrative part of her livelihood. For both clients, the rich colors helped them say, "This area is about wealth."

Symbols of Prosperity

The most powerful symbol of prosperity is an object that cost a lot of money. It can be as small as a stamp or as large as furniture. **Expensive objects** are the main things I recommend for this area. I collect bookends, and I'm happy to say I have a vintage Tiffany bookend in our Wealth Corner. My husband was visibly shocked when I told him how much I paid for it—his words still echo in my head: "You paid that much for a *bookend*?" The instant I heard that, I knew I'd bought the right bookend and put it in the right place, and I've certainly never regretted it. And he got over it when I showed him how much they're selling for on eBay.

The valuable object does not have to be visible. One client hid a ruby under the carpet of the house he had for sale. The house was empty and just sitting on the market. I went to the Wealth Corner of the home, which was in the master bedroom. I yanked up a very small area of carpet in the corner, and said, "Do you have anything valuable you can put here?" He said he had a ruby, and I replied, "Sir, if you're willing to put a ruby in this corner, I predict very good things." The place sold lickety-split, and the seller retrieved his ruby before escrow closed. Many people put expensive jewelry in their Wealth Corner, and that's perfect. Because costume jewelry is artificial, it would not be good in the Wealth Corner unless the jewelry is collectable and valuable in its own right.

Actual Money

Actual money kept in a Wealth Corner should be hundred-dollar bills or collectable currency worth at least that much. A piggy bank or big glass jug with coins inside is not appropriate in the Wealth Corner—it's small change. The money doesn't have be visible; it can be safely tucked away.

Representations of Money

Things that look like money, but that you can't really spend, are not recommended in the Wealth Corner. This includes objects with dollar signs as their design, as well as fake money, such as from board games or enlarged reproductions of paper money. Don't store bills that you owe or have paid in the Wealth Corner. They represent money leaving you.

Water

If possible, put a fountain in your Wealth Corner and *keep it going.* If you're willing to do that, you won't look back. Some feng shui consultants advise not having water or images of water in a bedroom. I've not seen a detrimental effect in people's lives when they have water images in their bedrooms—just don't overdo it by using water as the main decorative theme in the room. Here's my advice: When a bedroom is in the Wealth Corner of the whole house and whoever sleeps there doesn't mind the fountain going *all the time*, then consider installing one. Some people find that keeping a fountain going all the time is like having a pet because a fountain does require attention. What you never want in a Wealth Corner is a fountain that isn't circulating water—you would be sending a message opposite to the one you intend.

A woman took one of my classes on the bagua, and as a result she put a fountain in a corner of the large master bedroom, which was also the Wealth Corner of the whole house. Her husband pooh-poohed the idea, but within a week their coffee shop reached the daily sales goal they had set for it, but had never quite made. A few days later they exceeded the goal. The wife thought she'd have some fun with her previously doubting husband. She said, "I think you're right. I think the fountain had nothing to do with our record-setting days. I'm going to remove it." "Oh, no you don't!" was his response.

If you do have a fountain in the bedroom, feel free to turn it off at night, but use a timer so that it's already going when you get up in the morning. Fountain motors have very strong electromagnetic fields, which are bad for your health if you have prolonged exposure. Don't place a fountain within a yard of your body where you sleep or sit frequently.

An aquarium is also a nice addition in the Wealth Corner, or even a picture of water. A water image is my most frequent recommendation for Wealth Corners. If growing plants are shown in the picture, so much the better—that symbolizes your wealth growing. A picture showing fresh water is better than a picture of *only* ocean water because fresh water can *sustain* you and your vegetable garden.

Plants

Wood is the element for the Wealth Corner, and the best way to represent wood is with growing plants. Plants with stiff, pokey leaves are to be avoided. This also applies in the far left corner of your back yard. Dried plants are very bad in any part of the home because they say *dead*. They once had life energy coursing through them, but that life is gone, and they're now dead. Artificial plants don't have that problem because they were never alive. Just keep them clean and very realistically arranged. I mentioned a little earlier that an image of water and plants growing is ideal for Wealth Corners. For many people that is the most feasible thing to do. It's quite easy to find plant pictures, so keep looking until you find one that you like that *also* shows water.

The ideal living houseplants for the Money Corner have any of these four characteristics:

Round-Leaf Succulent

The round shape says that the plant is approachable. The succulent aspect symbolizes prosperity because the leaves are fat with water, and water symbolizes wealth. Most succulents need direct sun or they become leggy, so if your Wealth Corner gets lots of sun, jade plant is a perfect choice. Don't select thorny cactus or pointy-leaf succulents for this area. Certain cactus, such as Christmas cactus, are fine here because they don't have thorns. The flowers should be a rich red, rather than pink, because this is the area for rich colors.

Expensive and Elegant

Any expensive plant is good in the Wealth Corner, but it's ideal if the plant is expensive *and* elegant. An extremely expensive African violet would be appropriate, especially if the flower color is a deep, rich tone. But it's even better if the plant *looks* expensive to almost anyone. Tall plants are generally excellent in this area but make sure they don't actually touch the ceiling because that says you've reached your limit. Palms are unmistakably elegant and very appropriate here, especially the expensive lady palm (*Rhapis excelsia*). Consider a variegated lady palm if you can find (and afford) one, but make sure it has a distinct variegation, not a blurry variegation. If your budget won't stretch quite that far, parlor palm (*Chamaedora elegans*) is also fine. It's also known as neanthe bella and although it doesn't get as tall as most lady palms, it seldom needs repotting and is perhaps the most durable of all indoor palms. These two palms can grow without direct sun and are fairly trouble-free, which is important because sick or dying plants are sending the absolutely *wrong message*. And you certainly don't want to spend a lot of money on a plant if you're not confident you can keep it alive.

Plants That Remind You of Money

Leaves can look like coins or they can look like paper money. Paper money is my favorite, but coins are better than nothing. *Dieffenbachia species* (also called dumb cane) has large dark green leaves with spots of white that are reminiscent of large paper currency. Jade plant (*Crassula ovata*) and its close relative silver dollar plant (*Crassula arborescens*) have rounded fat leaves which are like big coins, so they are good in the Wealth Corner.

Purple Plants

Plants with purple leaves or flowers are excellent in the Wealth Corner. Any African violet that has richly colored flowers is excellent, with purple or violet being the ideal colors. Purple wandering Jew (*Tradescantia zebrina* or *T. pallida*) is easy to grow with adequate sun and water. Velvet plant (*Gynura aurantiaca*), which was also recommended for the Relationship Corner, has beautiful soft, purple hairs and is good in the Wealth Corner as well. Plants with rich red or blue flowers are also excellent.

Windows and Mirrors

Windows in the Wealth Corner are a potential problem because they represent opportunities for your wealth energy to leave the home. Put a clear, faceted crystal in the windows. The crystal symbolizes your wish that the wealth energy be dispersed back into the home before it leaves too quickly. Say out loud words to that effect. The crystal can sit on a ledge or hang. It could even be incorporated into a stained glass artwork. Don't use small, inexpensive crystals for this purpose in the Wealth Corner. Use the largest crystal that will *look appropriate* in the window.

If the window gets direct sunlight, use an octagonal crystal, rather than a disco-ball shaped crystal, because the octagon shape makes much larger rainbows of color. If the crystal is hanging, make sure that it can't touch the glass, even in a sudden draft of wind. Lead crystal is softer than glass and the crystal (not the window) will chip if it knocks against the glass. Once the crystal is chipped, it's no longer appropriate for the Wealth Corner because it is a broken object. Some consultants recommend hanging crystals with red thread; however, I use clear monofilament, such as fishing line, to hang crystals. My reason is that the crystal is the important thing, not what it hangs from.

You could also use sheer curtains over the windows, but they should be made of expensive material, such as silk or real handmade lace. Window treatments in the Wealth Corner should be as lavish as is appropriate for your style. My favorite window treatment in this area is a layered look—nice sheers with heavy drapes that are pulled to the side in the day and closed at night. Part of the extravagance of the drapes should be an excess of fabric, where some of it puddles on the floor. Drapes that puddle on the floor are used in feng shui to pull energy *upward*, which is almost always a good direction to move energy.

Mirrors represent windows—not the tiny coin-size mirrors, but regular-size mirrors in which you can easily see yourself. It's best to avoid having large mirrors in the Wealth Corner since they represent opportunities for wealth energy to leak away.

Other Holes in the Wall

Holes in the wall are also opportunities for energy to leak away, so spackle over any miscellaneous holes that have been left by pins, nails or screws.

Another way that energy can leak out of a home is through wall sockets. If something is plugged into the socket, there is no leak, but if the holes are visible there is leakage. In some homes when the weather is cold, you can feel cold air seeping in through bare sockets on outside walls. That's not energy coming in—that's your money going out via your heating bill. The solution is simple—use opaque socket protectors or covers, the kind that prevent babies from sticking things into the sockets. Often, the socket covers are translucent, and those aren't best for feng shui purposes. Opaque ones are better, preferably in the same color as the socket plate.

Wealth Corner of Back Yard

The far left corner of your back yard is also a Wealth Corner and should be maintained with special care. Make it inviting with plantings or a decorative object (such as a purple gazing ball) that draws the eye. Do not keep your garbage cans here, but it is fine to have a compost bin—you are making rich soil. One of my California clients had a locked shipping container permanently parked in the Wealth Corner of her back yard. She said it was full of old files and records, but that she had lost the key years ago. She was having a lot of trouble decluttering her home, and the stagnation in the Wealth Corner of her yard was exacerbating the situation. The feng shui solution in a case like that is a call to the locksmith.

Bathroom in Wealth Corner

A Wealth Corner bathroom is a problem because there are several drains in the room, each one symbolizing money draining away. A center bathroom is the only location that's worse, and that's discussed in the final chapter.

There are several symbolic fixes for a bathroom in a Wealth Corner, and the first four fixes are also for use in homes with a center bathroom.

Door Closed

If the door is kept closed when no one is coming or going, then the energy in the rest of the home won't even find the bathroom in your Money Area. Instead of nagging others in the household to close the door, I suggest installing a hinge pin closer on one of the door hinges. The door will then gently close itself. Because occasionally the door *has* to be opened, the second fix is needed.

Bagua Mirror

Mount a bagua mirror on the wall above the door going into the bathroom. The mirror goes *outside* the bathroom. Its purpose is to reflect away the energy of the home so that it doesn't enter the bathroom, especially during times that the door has to be open, such as after a steamy shower. There's often a thin blue plastic film over the mirror surface for protection against scratches in the store—remove that film before installing the mirror.

A correct bagua mirror has *I Ching* trigrams on each of the eight sides of the frame. Those trigrams are three lines with some solid (yang) and some broken (yin), and they are positioned to symbolize *perfect balance*. A bathroom in a

Wealth Corner is an out-of-order situation, and the images on the frame symbolize that things are now back in perfect order or balance. In *Feng Shui and Your Health*, Jes Lim points out that another symbol of perfect balance is the Seal of Solomon; you can put a mirror in the center of it and use it instead of a bagua mirror. (See Sources.)

The Seal of Solomon has been used by many cultures to indicate balance. It can be used instead of a bagua mirror.

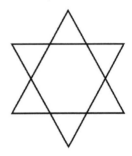

Tiny Wind Chimes

Hang a very tiny wind chime inside the bathroom so the top of the door barely touches the bottom clapper of the chime. It can be hung from a bracket above the door or from the ceiling. It should be only four to six inches away from the wall so the door touches the wind chime every time it opens. The immediate sound from above counters the down-draining vibration of the room.

Upward Objects

Upward pointed objects, such as obelisks, aim energy upward, and that's ideal in any bathroom because much of the energy in the room is going downward. The plant *Sansevieria trifascata*, also known as mother-in-law's tongue or snake plant, is good in any bathroom. The leaves point upward and don't splay out to point at people. Most plant stores have the tall-size plants, but they're also available in a short or squat size, which is more appropriate in small bathrooms. Since it's the Wealth Corner, you might splurge and get the kind with pure white variegation called Bantel's

Sensation. It's not common, but worth the extra expense especially since it's so durable that you're not likely to kill it, even in low light conditions.

Green Color and Plant Imagery

Wood, the feng shui element in the Wealth Corner, is considered to control the element water because plant roots suck up water. Wood is represented by the color green and the shape of vertical rectangles. Pictures of plants are good in bathrooms, as are living plants.

Additional Considerations

Be sure to put in place the fixes for drains, which were mentioned in the preceding chapter. And since this is the Wealth Corner, it's helpful if the bathroom and accessories are expensive and in the correct colors for the area. Don't overdo decorative objects in any bathroom; that type of decorating is yin, and bathrooms are already too yin because water is a yin element.

Missing Wealth Corner

A missing Wealth Corner is **really bad news**. I've counseled many prospective buyers against purchasing homes that have the far left corner missing. Those homes are usually a bargain because the current owner is *having* to sell at a loss. The new buyer then inherits that energy of financial decline because the shape of the home calls for it. If you can feasibly enlarge your home to include that corner, I urge you to do so. That's not usually possible, so the good news is that there *are* symbolic cures, and they are mostly the same as described in Chapter Three for missing Relationship Corners. The main difference is that at the apex of the missing Wealth Corner, you should put something expensive. Use *pairs* for the Relationship Corner, and for the missing Wealth Corner use an *expensive object*. Also, when using mirrors inside to bring back the missing Wealth Corner, don't use large mirrors—instead, use very small mirrors. Remember that mirrors represent windows and windows in the Wealth Corner are an opportunity for wealth energy to leak away.

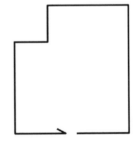

Prosperity will be elusive in a home with this shape.

If the apex of the missing Wealth Corner is in the yard, it's best to put a significant object there to mark the corner. Examples are: a light (which needs to be turned on at least once a month), a fountain (kept going), a birdbath (maintained with fresh water) or a sculpture (not too small, and not too cheap). It needs to be a made object (because the house is a made object), so a plant is not the best way to mark the missing corner. At one consultation, the family rented the house, and the landlord mowed the lawn, so the object to bring back the missing Wealth Corner had to be buried. The wife chose to bury a bracelet of semiprecious stones that she had inherited from her mother. The next time I consulted for them, it was at the home they had bought in the most expensive neighborhood in town. I knew how much houses cost in that area, and I was quite amazed. If you bury an expensive object, make sure it is protected well.

It's particularly difficult to properly bring back a missing corner when the apex is at the bottom of a swimming pool. A client on O'ahu had exactly that situation, but her husband was a diver, and he had no problem putting something at the bottom of the pool. He took an amethyst ring that she had inherited from her mother, and to protect it he glued a ceramic cup of the sort used to cover the bolts holding a toilet. He didn't believe in feng shui, but he loved his wife and was willing to humor her. His dive business was part of a national franchise, and he soon got a call from the head office, "What are you doing there? The economy's awful, and all the other locations are doing terribly, but you folks are doing great!" He became such a believer that he asked me to feng shui his office. I've had clients with swimming pools at the apex of missing Wealth Corners who have *not* followed my suggestions, and their lives are expressing *wealth draining away.* ✍

Chapter Six

Career and Fame Areas

Two other bagua areas also greatly concern money—the Career Area and the Fame Area. They are directly across from each other, with the middle third of the far wall being the Fame Area; fire is its element. The middle third of the entrance wall (the wall with the entrance door on it) is the Career Area, more properly known as the Life's Path Area; water is the element here.

Career Area

The Career Area is about the entire flow of your life, not just what you do for employment, but it *also* concerns your career. The Career Area is the most yin of all the bagua areas.

Water

Water is the element in this area, so having real water is ideal. The water can be moving or still. If a fountain seems appealing in your situation, be sure to read the precautions below about fountains. The direction of the flow is crucial—the water should look as though it's aimed toward the heart of the home. It's also fine to have a fountain that flows in all directions like an umbrella.

Early in my feng shui career I spoke at a bookstore in Sacramento. Months later, a woman called telling me that she had attended that talk and put a fountain in her Career Area and had gotten fired the same day. "Tell me more," I said. She said, "It was one of those fountains with a light under the water, and it had a little stone ball that was supposed to go round and round—but that part never worked."

I hadn't yet learned that any time I say the word "fountain" I have to immediately say a few more words regarding them. **Fountains only work when they are properly running. Never choose a fountain with a lightbulb below the water.** A lightbulb under the water says *conflict* because fire and water are opposing elements, and this setup places them too close together. Nature gives us the sun shining down on water, so it's fine to have a fountain with a light above the water.

If you have a fountain you have to keep it going. A dry fountain says, "Dried up, broken, doesn't work—nothing happening here." Only when a fountain is turned on and in good working order is it sending out its very positive message: "Good fortune is bubbling up all the time." The fountain can be turned off when everyone is gone or sleeping. The best fountain maintains a visible pool of water, even when it's turned off, rather than letting the water vanish under pebbles into a reservoir.

Here's another experience I learned from: One of my clients had a very small office at work, and we were trying to find a way to put a waterfall image in the Career Area. The door to the office took up the entire middle third of the entrance wall, and she kept the door open most of the time, so there was no place to put a picture. I reluctantly suggested that she put a waterfall picture in the small space above the door. I warned her this was something I hadn't tried before, and I wasn't confident of what the results would be. I said, "This could very well symbolize that your good fortune is going *out* the door."

Indeed, that's exactly what happened. She called again after a few weeks, saying her boss was giving her a very hard time. I said, "Take the waterfall down immediately. And if we're going to get a waterfall anywhere in your Career Area it has to be under the carpet." She was able to discreetly pull up enough carpet to put a super-small picture of water that looked as if it was flowing from the door into the office. Within a week she notified me that her boss was now praising her highly. Any flowing water image in the Career Area should show the water flowing *into* the room, not out the door.

One of my clients had a black candle with the word "water" on it in the Career Area. I explained that just because something is marketed as a feng shui item doesn't mean it actually functions as such. The lure of feng shui is sometimes used to sell products that are designed by people with no deep knowledge of feng shui rules. Fire and water are the most opposite elements, and their combination in the candle was not auspicious—the burning of the candle would destroy the word "water."

The shape that represents water is wavy or free-form because water can take any shape. Free-form glass objects are very appropriate here.

Other Enhancements

Black or **dark blue** are excellent colors for the Career Area because they represent Water. If you paint an accent wall black, never buy the generic black that's on the shelf in the paint store. Pick a black that harmonizes with your existing colors by selecting from a paint chip fan deck from one or more paint companies. **White** also works in the Career Area because it's the color that represents metal, and metal is seen to create water, just as water forms on the outside of a metal pipe.

Frank Lloyd Wright had the correct idea by creating foyers with lower than average ceilings, then raising the ceiling as you walk on into the home. Cozy foyers are yin and very appropriate in homes. A double-height foyer is too yang for what is always a yin area of the bagua. The too-high ceiling should be painted a darker color than the walls to make it appear lower. Crown molding also helps and it, too, should be darker than the walls.

Fame Area

The Fame Area is the most yang bagua area. It is a *very important area* for people who need fame to earn their living—artists, actors and authors, for example. Those who just want a good reputation, but aren't looking for fame, don't have to do as much in this area, just some. If you need fame, feel free to decorate this area boldly with the following suggestions in mind.

Fire

Fire is the element for the Fame Area, so it would seem that this is an appropriate area for a fireplace or candles. However, a fireplace says *fire* only when a fire is burning there. Otherwise, it says *earth* if the fireplace is stone or brick—or *metal* if it's made of metal. Candles say fire only when they are lit.

Red

Red is the ideal color to represent fire, but it should not be an earthy, orangey red like terracotta, because orange-red represents the element earth. People are often loath to paint red on a wall in their home, but it does have impact.

I consulted for Hawai'i Island artist Ira Ono, whose Fame Area was in his laundry room. I said, "Nobody will notice if this room is red." He agreed, and made it red. A few weeks later he called early in the morning, "Have you seen today's paper?" I said, "No, not yet." He said, "I'm on the cover in color!" One of his ornaments was going to appear on the White House Christmas tree. If you need fame for your livelihood, find a way to incorporate red in this area. It doesn't have to be paint—it can be fabric or other red objects.

Animal Imagery or Material

Animals (including people) are fiery because they have the fire of life. Objects made from animals, such as leather, fur, bones and feathers, are appropriate here. Pictures or figurines of people or animals are also good here. The animals that best represent fire are birds because they move so quickly—red birds, such as cardinals, being ideal. Animals that live under water, such as dolphins, are not appropriate.

Angular Shape

Angular objects are good in the Fame Area, as long as the points don't aim at people, so things that point directly up are best. Examples are metronomes, obelisks and pointed lamp finials.

Many plants have angular leaves, but inside your home, leaves with sharp points that aim at you (like pineapple tops) are not good feng shui. Mother-in-law's tongue (*Sansevieria trifascata*) was recommended earlier as a good plant for bathrooms because the leaves aim only upwards, not outward. It's also great in the Fame Area because the leaves symbolize flames going up.

Electricity

Electrical items are considered fiery and are appropriate in the Fame Area. However, be considerate of the earth, and don't waste electricity.

Plastic

Plastic is considered fiery and yang. I don't encourage buying more plastic, but we've all got some so it's good to know where to put it—in the Fame Area. It does not have to be on display; it can be in a drawer or cabinet.

Wood and Plants

Wood feeds a fire and is therefore an excellent symbol in the Fame area. Wood can be represented by houseplants, artificial plants, pictures of plants and wooden furniture or objects. Vertical lines represent tree trunks growing upward and are likewise good in the Fame Area. A suggestion for an easy-to-grow houseplant for this area is the jewel orchid (*Ludisia discolor*). It looks striking year-round because there's some red on both sides of the variegated leaves.

Missing Areas

If part or all of the Fame or Career Areas is missing, use mirrors to symbolically enlarge the house. The mirrors can be placed on any or all of the walls that are tangent to the missing area, with the reflective side of the mirror shining into the room. Large mirrors are preferred, but often not feasible, so it's fine to use small mirrors. ❧

The home on the left has a missing Career Area, and the home on the right has a missing Fame Area.

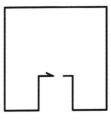 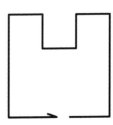

Chapter Seven

Center Bathroom

A center bathroom does not have to be smack-dab in the center of the home. Any bathroom that does not have an outside wall as one of its walls is considered a center bathroom.

The Worst Problem

I saved the worst 'til last. A center bathroom in a home is the absolute worst thing I know of in feng shui. This observation is based on much personal experience—some of it my own. Way back when I was single and looking, I thought I'd found the right person for me. The house we moved into together had a bathroom that was almost in the exact center of the square building. When my partner and I went to look at the home for the first time, it looked like pigs lived there. The husband slept in one bedroom, and his wife and her boyfriend slept in the other bedroom. They had tried to buy the house, but weren't able to keep up with their payments, so we ended up buying the house from the man who had originally built it. And he had gone bankrupt in the process. That relationship lasted only six months—I didn't know to beware of center bathrooms and predecessor energy.

I speak with a lot of conviction when I caution against center bathrooms. Fairly early in my feng shui career, a woman called me to consult for her home in South San Francisco. When I arrived, she was there with her mother, who also lived in the home. As we walked toward the back of the house, I noticed a very dark bathroom to my left. I said, "It looks like we've got a serious problem, so we'd better stop and talk about it. This bathroom doesn't have an outside window, and no sides touch an outside wall of the house, so it's called a center bathroom. That represents disease, divorce and bankruptcy." The mother started jumping up and down pointing to the floor. "That's this house, that's this house!" she kept saying. The daughter got a bit teary and said that she was indeed going through bankruptcy and divorce at the same time, and she had just been diagnosed with breast cancer.

In the first ten or so years of my feng shui practice, I used to tell my clients that a center bathroom meant disease, divorce or bankruptcy. But now I have regretfully added a fourth word to that litany—death. I had a good friend who was an architect. When I first consulted for him, he and his partner were living in a two-story home that he had designed. Each floor had a center bathroom. My advice went unheeded, and his partner soon left him. A couple of years later, he showed me plans for the new home he was hoping to build for himself and his new partner. Smack in the middle of the house were two bathrooms, side by side. I told him what a horrible idea I thought that was, and his exact words were, "But that won't affect me will it?" I was dumfounded and, for once, at a loss for words. I just couldn't believe what I'd heard. Well, he moved into the home while it was still under construction (never a good idea), and one day he was working on the roof when his head started to feel funny. His partner took him to the doctor; he was rushed to the closest big hospital and was dead the next day.

Identifying a Center Bathroom

As long as what's on the other side of the wall is **outside** your home, it is not a center bathroom. If a neighbor's unit is on the opposite side, that is considered an outside wall because what's on the other side of the wall is outside of your home. A skylight does not mitigate the effects of a center bathroom. A skylight improves the vibration of any bathroom and helps plants grow, but it *doesn't change the location* of the bathroom.

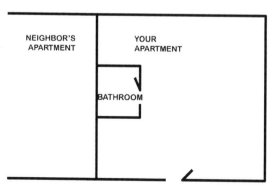

NEIGHBOR'S APARTMENT

YOUR APARTMENT

BATHROOM

This bathroom is considered to touch an outside wall because the neighbor's apartment is directly adjacent.

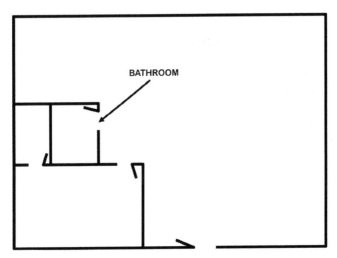

This bathroom does not touch an outside wall so it is considered a center bathroom, even though it is not in the exact center of the home.

Fixes

The real fixes for a center bathroom are to remove the bathroom or move—those are by far your best options. Since they aren't immediately feasible for most people in this situation, there are symbolic fixes.

Implement the first four fixes in the Bathroom in Wealth Corner section in Chapter Five. Also, put a mirror on the outside of the bathroom door—the bigger the better. Make sure the mirror is securely fastened and does not rattle. Don't forget to keep this door, like all bathroom doors, closed as often as possible. For color in a center bathroom use *earth tones, including yellow.* Decorate sparingly using primarily *pottery* or *stone.* ☙

Recommended Reading

I knew I was doing my feng shui correctly when I got Watermark Publishing as a publisher. First of all, their name is quite auspicious for a feng shui author, and they really know how to create fabulous books. Please check out my two previous books from Watermark Publishing, **Feng Shui for Hawai'i** (the third printing is by far the best edition) and **Feng Shui for Hawai'i Gardens**. Even though "Hawai'i" is in the titles, the information is applicable everywhere, and they're both chock full of color drawings and photographs. Many of the non-bagua related topics in this book are discussed in more depth in those two books. Color pictures are included as *practical instruction*, and the captions explain how to evaluate what you're seeing. The books are available at stores, through bookshawaii.net or by calling 1-866-900-BOOK.

If your income depends on a retail store, you couldn't do better than to read my **Feng Shui for Retail Stores**. Retail is second nature to me. I began working in stores when I was fifteen and opened my first of three bookstores when I was nineteen. In addition to providing information about the physical layout, I give careful, specific instructions about how to treat customers in person or over the phone. In feng shui that's called *greeting chi energy,* and it's as vital as the merchandise your store carries.

Ten years after my first two books—**Feng Shui Demystified** and **Bedroom Feng Shui**—were published, I reissued them in revised, expanded editions. Both books explain more about the bagua, covering all nine bagua areas. My books are available in five languages and can be ordered through any bookstore or online.

Feng Shui for Relationships by Gerry Heaton is by far the best and most useful book about the Relationship Corner. It's uncomplicated, easy to read, and full of details. Heaton's writing is delightful and full of common sense. He gives you a good feel for the whole of feng shui while concentrating on the Relationship Corner.

This book has much substance and yet is inviting for a quick browse. It's brimming with tables describing situations and classifying them as "good" or "not so good" for relationship energy. For instance, if the Relationship Corner of the home happens to be a "room that is left vacant or unused, this symbolizes the neglect of your talents and of your relationships."

One of the author's greatest services is his insistence on the power of pink to stimulate good relationship energy. He acknowledges that many men have a problem with this advice. His suggestion is to "add the merest touch of red to a huge can of white paint, and the paint will take on a very, very subtle pink tinge. It can be so subtle that it would only be detected by placing pure white next to it. The effect, however, is quite amazing—the human eye can detect the subtle amount of warmth that is associated with love energy."

The book may not be readily available in bookstores because it's published in Australia, but you can order it through Pacific Island Books, 303-920-8338, pacificislandbooks.com.

The kind of feng shui I practice (Form School, or Landform) is based on what things are shaped like and their symbolism. There is another kind of feng shui, which uses the cardinal directions (north, south, east, west) as a basis for its advice. Two of the most pertinent books which base their advice on the compass are also simple to read: Angi Ma Wong's *Feng Shui Dos & Taboos for Love* and *Feng Shui Dos & Taboos for Financial Success*.

If you want to grow scented plants in your Relationship Corner there are two very good guides: ***The Essence of Paradise*** by Tovah Martin for indoor plants and ***A Garden of Fragrance*** by Suzy Bales for outdoors. If these books are difficult to find, try bookfinder.com, which is my favorite source for out-of-print books.

Perfect Health by Deepak Chopra has the simplest test of any book I know of for determining your ayurvedic body type. Most skinny people are vata. I should know: My father was a featherweight boxer, and my mother considers 110 pounds to be a healthy weight for herself. I'm naturally skinny and I'll testify—skinny people should not attempt living in places with constant strong winds, especially if the wind is cold—it unbalances us. Pitta people do well in a cool environment, and kapha people benefit from dry heat. Whatever your weight and size, I recommend knowing which of the three ayurvedic body types (called doshas) you are. You'll then know why certain environments simply *feel right* for your body. This book is easy to find in any library or bookstore.

I'm fascinated by color and its influence. Recently I read two wonderful books, which relate to two of the colors I recommend in this book: pink and red. The power of red is brilliantly and uniquely discussed in ***Through the Language Glass: Why the World Looks Different in Other Languages*** by Guy Deutscher. Pink is discussed in ***Drunk Tank Pink: And Other Unexpected Forces That Shape How We Think, Feel, and Behave*** by Adam Alter. He explains the ability of pink to disempower men.

Lastly, I'd like to highly recommend ***Why Men Don't Listen and Women Can't Read Maps: How We're Different & What To Do About It*** by Barbara and Allan Pease. Whether you're gay or straight, woman or man, *everybody* who has or is looking for a spouse should read this book. Even if you're single and happy that way, this book will help you understand yourself better. ✐

From Watermark Publishing

Feng Shui for Hawai'i
by Clear Englebert

A variety of creative feng shui solutions for different tastes and budgets.

"Has universal appeal for those wanting to learn more about feng shui."
—Carole Hyder, *Conversations with Your Home*

Softcover; 152 pp

Also available in e-reader format on Amazon and the Apple iBookstore.

Feng Shui for Hawai'i Gardens
by Clear Englebert

Invite good energy into your home, balance your home in its surroundings and protect it from harsh or threatening energies.

"Practical and aesthetic advice...all worth taking."
—Made Wijaya, *Tropical Garden Design*

Softcover; 216 pp

Sources

Bagua Mirrors

These are available in most Chinese dry goods stores or from online sources such as eBay. The mirror in the center is either convex, concave or flat. For inside a home, I usually recommend the flat or convex mirrors.

Crystals

Make sure these are completely clear, not tinted or iridescent. They are sometimes available in Chinese dry goods stores or bead shops. Mine came from Xinacat.com—the 8015 and 8115 octagon series are the best prismatically.

Edge Guards for Bare Glass

Brandsport (541-341-6555) has flexible plastic molding intended for car doors which works perfectly for edging bare glass edges, if the glass is not very thick. It comes in every conceivable color and then some. Brandsport.com/ptrm-140c-05.html shows the product and brandsport.com/prtrcoma.html shows all the colors.

Hinge Pin Closer

There are several types of these door closers. They are small, simple to install and available at any hardware store.

Seal of Solomon Mirrors

The shape represents perfect balance. The mirrors sold at Lavender Moon Gallery (808-324-7708, lavendermoongallery.com) are designed by Dianne McMillen and are surrounded by stained glass lotus frames in a choice of colors. You can also make your own Seal of Solomon mirror by drawing or etching the design onto any mirror.

Tiny Mirrors

These are available inexpensively in craft stores.

Tiny Wind Chimes

Karizma, 415-861-4515, karizma1@att.net

They are an excellent source for tiny wind chimes.

White Sage

White sage is often available in natural food stores. But remember, it's not culinary sage.

Index

Bold page numbers refer to the most complete information on the topic. The books and authors in Recommended Reading are not included in the index.

About the Author

Clear Englebert is the author of six highly praised books on feng shui. They are available in five languages. His next book will be *Feng Shui Outside* and his future book plans include *Feng Shui with House Plants* and *Feng Shui for Collectors*. (If you're a collector he's looking for photos of collections.) He lives in Hawai'i and teaches and consults throughout the state. Visit his website fungshway.com.

Made in the USA
San Bernardino, CA
09 February 2016